T0065189

FAIRLY AVENUE

HASNAA ELNAGDY

ARCHWAY
PUBLISHING

Archway Publishing books may be ordered through booksellers or by contacting:

Archway Publishing
1663 Liberty Drive
Bloomington, IN 47403
www.archwaypublishing.com
844-669-3957

ISBN: 978-1-6657-5041-7 (sc)
ISBN: 978-1-6657-5042-4 (e)

Library of Congress Control Number: 2023918175

Print information available on the last page.

Archway Publishing rev. date: 09/25/2023

In the name of Allah

CONTENTS

PREFACE

Freedom is pleasant feelings. How can people gain personal freedom? How can they manage the distress? This book includes a list of skills that people need to overcome the solid barriers of anguish and accomplish their goals. People love to reach their goals, but sometimes the doors seem closed. Some people feel unhappy because they live in their inner prisons of self-blame. They strive for perfection and power. How can people reach a safe river's trail to the fair avenue of peace? In this book, the readers will find useful notions and inner respite, with coping skills to support himself or herself in dealing with hardship. In fact, if an individual has distress from various reasons, such as loss of a job, chronic illness, or loss of loved one, he or she may suffer from dysfunctional performances. Additionally, the individual might run in a fantasy circle, which was surrounded by circular barriers. This book contains recommendations of researchers. Basically, peace is a basic source of happiness. There are several types of peace, such as peace with family members, peace with friends, peace among coworkers, and peace on the earth. How can an individual have all types of peace, all the time? This book offers suggestions for empowerment and motivation. It also includes real stories of messengers of the creator of the universe and how they overcame distress.

CHAPTER 1

River's Trail

MOST PEOPLE HOPE TO BE WELL REGARDED BY OTHERS. IF AN INDIVIDUAL believes in the destructive points of view of others, he or she will have distress. Some parents' points of views cause children to have bad self-images. Many people are affected by unpleasant feelings of shame and guilt. People internalize the images of their ideal individuals, such as teachers, uncles. Some of them withdraw and withhold from their surrounding environment. They isolate themselves to feel secure. They put imaginary safeguards around themselves to prevent any relationships from interacting. They place rules on themselves to stay away from others. In fact, they make false decisions when they substitute the outer problem by using something else to alleviate their distress. It is unwise to numb their unwanted feelings by abusing addictive substances, such as alcohol, drugs, or gambling. Those people feel unhappy because they live in their inner prisons of self-blame. They strive for perfection and power. They think their defects cannot be healed, and they will never be accepted by themselves or by others, but family caring, and empathy helps to heal the disowned self from shame and guilt.

In overwhelming situations, the individual may have distress over responsibilities. Sometimes, he or she has distress for various reasons such as: loss of a job, chronic illness, loss of loved one, or divorce. He or she may feel as if is drowning in a flood. And he or she may feel like ground meat because of the loss of valuable things. On top of that he or she may suffer from dysfunctional performances when distress increases because of passionate agonies that he or she may not know how to deal with that. The individual should know the reasons for his or her current distress in the here and now. People do not like to miss anything, but it is often out of their hands. The individual should use rational thinking to feel comfort and to try to adjust to the situations gradually.

During perplexing time, there is always an internal dialogue that directs the individual's personal behavior toward pleasures or perfectionism. Naturally, the response should have a balance between the desire of pleasure and correctness. He or she should stick by safe thinking to walk from a dark avenue to the bright fair avenue.

The joy from family and friends happens for a limited time. After that, people look for other ways to have the fantastic feeling of continuous joy. Some people use extra entertainment, or they abuse food, drugs, or alcohol. They might have addictive relationships, or they may smoke tobacco. They might be a workaholic or player of gambling. Addictive substances produce a temporary feeling of relief. These people then get overwhelmed by the negative consequences of their actions. They become tired and fed up with the ways of fun, and they look for another way.

Money may be a reason for distress. No one can buy true love with money or worldly treasures. Once people need money, they waste their time in searching for it. If they are rich, they waste their time collecting more money. In fact, when people die, they cannot use or take money with them.

Personal freedom is a hope, it produces pleasant feelings. How can the individual have personal freedom? When parents overwatch family members, this limits the family member's personal freedom and may cause conflicts. Stopping interference in others' personal issues is one reason for happiness. The family system should offer chances for the family members to decide what should be done.

The loss of imaginary boundaries between family members may cause problems. Flexible boundaries diminish conflicts, enhance good relationships, and reinforce respect. Hence, personal freedom can be gained with wisdom because freedom without moral direction transforms to corruption. In addition, micromanagement and harsh communication may turn family members into enemies. Unequal treatment of siblings or parental bias toward one of the children may also cause envy or rage. Empathy and compassion are the main sources of love between family members.

Peace and resilience are also great sources of satisfaction. There are several types of peace. Peace with family members or peace with friends might mean stable relationships, which continue to flourish and prosper. Peace among coworkers helps people become more artistic, creative, motivated, and cooperative at their jobs. Peace on earth refers to having safety from pandemics, natural disasters, severe weather, or pollution. All people want to have safety from epidemic disease, crime, poverty, violence, and war. They do not like the loss of a loved one or divorce. How can all these types of peace be available to all people all the time? Walking on the fair avenue with peace alleviates sorrow and inserts hopes. Hope strength toward achieving goals. Some hope might take place, while the rest do not.

The regulation of the universe is out of human hands. For example, they can't control the weather, nor prevent natural disasters, or stop a rupture of stars or the rupture of an asteroid. They can't stop the sun from rising in the east or stop the illumination of the moon at night.

The main source of peace is the recognition of a higher power. He is the creator of the universe. The individual should check his or her beliefs. Self-awareness and self-exploration of values and beliefs are essential for joy and happiness. Some people have shame and guilt because they do not practice any religion, or they do not practice the right way of worshipping. Empowering heavenly religions of faith encourages and maintains personal insight and awareness. The river's trail to the righteous is safe to reach the fair avenue of peace.

The rejecters

Those who reject a belief in the higher power should ask themselves the following questions:

- Can any creature control the weather or the solar system? No, there is *not* any creature that can control the weather or the solar system.
- How is the solar system controlled while people are busy?
- Who does keep the body's organs working, including the hearts and lungs, while they are sleeping?
- Who does send intense winds, which move the clouds above them?
- Who does provide natural rain?
- Who does keep the earth at a perfect distance from the sun to prevent freezing or burning?
- Who does raise the skies without columns?
- Who does give the birds the knowledge to migrate?
- Who does create live cells from water?
- Who does create humans and gives them the senses of hearing, vision, smell, taste, and touch?

It is impossible for any person on the earth to have all these valuable elements simultaneously without the help of a higher power—the creator of the universe. Some people may say it's nature, but nature cannot regulate the universe. The creator of the universe regulates the heavens, the earth, and everything in between.

According to the writing of David Capuzzi and Douglas R. Gross (2005), the high level of wellness in our lives comes from satisfying basic spiritual needs. This means empowering a love of God and having a belief that provides the sense of life. This initiates a love of values, integrity, and justice and discovering the inner wisdom and awareness of self. We need spirituality to heal the painful wounds of anguish, guilt, resentment, unforgiveness, and self-rejection. And we need spirituality to increase feelings of self-trust, self-esteem, hope, joy, and love of living (P. 253-254).

Complete healing of physical pain, emotional suffering, and sorrow needs the help of a higher power, the creator of the universe. Indeed, every person needs to have belief. The believers in the most merciful knew that he can help people to manage their lives. He can help addicts and alcoholics restore their rationality and to get back to their normal lives. The creator of the universe, the most merciful, is the real higher power. He can heal and cure illness. For example, in cases of cancer metastasis or loss of a loved one, deep-faith prayers may alleviate grief for some people and decrease suffering of symptoms.

Love can build pleasant characters and make people more optimistic and motivated. The real love between a man and a woman causes attraction between them without materialistic goals. This attraction is like trapped iron on the magnetic field. The future is in the knowledge of the creator of the universe. The love between a man and a woman may present pleasant memories, flashbacks, symbolic gifts, or unfinished business. The good memories come from thinking of happy times. The honest love between a man and a woman can survive if they marry during their lives on earth and will remarry in the hereafter in an eternal garden.

In the heavenly religions, there is a promise of the rewards of the eternal gardens to those whom the creator of the universe chooses. In the eternal gardens, the individual can have what he or she loves, such as a lovely spouse, free housing, or free supplies of food, drink, clothing, jewelry, plants, furniture, transportation, or shade. Personal hopes can be extended from the earth to the sky. Everyone has a definite and exciting goal. Personal hopes can survive in the eternal garden, which was designed as equal in width to the earth and the seven heavens.

Millions of people know there is only one real higher power or the creator of the universe. He manages people's lives and watches people, but people cannot see him. The real higher power is the best one who grants joy, hope, and motivation. He created the earth and everything natural and in between. He created the brains of the people who design and manufacture synthetic items and technology. People help each other by his permission, such as medical providers, farmers, engineers, soldiers, journalists, teachers, counselors, nurses, politicians, cashiers, bakers, law enforcement teams, and veterans.

People around the world have different beliefs or religions. The unworldly people love the creator of the universe more than anything because it is an eternal love, although the other types of love can vanish by breaking up or death. The believers know that it is impossible to feel joy without the help of the creator of the universe. Reading and listening to the stories of the messenger and prophets of the creator of the universe gives direction to rational thinking and rational behavior. The following chapters offer the real stories of the messengers and prophets of the creator of the universe, which include explanations of how they overcame distress.

CHAPTER 2

Miracles of Establishment of the Universe

THE STORIES OF THE CREATION OF THE UNIVERSE AND THE FIRST HUMAN (Adam) are according to the interpretation of Islamic resources. In Islam, Allah is the creator of universe.

> What is the meaning of the creation of the universe?
> It means creation of the heavens, earth, and everything in-between by Allah, the creator of the universe.

> Where was the first throne of Allah, the creator of the universe?
> The first throne of Allah was on the water's surface, such as oceans.

What did Allah, the creator of the universe, establish?

[Your Guardian-Lord is Allah, who created the heavens and the earth in six days, and is finally established on the throne (of authority): He draws the night as a veil over the day, each seeking the other in rapid succession: He created the sun, the moon, and the star, (all) governed by laws

under His Command (The Quran Translation, Ali, Yusuf 2007, 7:54)].

In six days, Allah created the seven heavens, earth, and everything in between. He created his throne of authority on the highest place of seventh heaven. He created heavens without pillars. He decorated the sky with the lights of stars and provided it with guards. He created the darkness of the night, the brightness of the day, the sun, and the moon. All of these are moving in big circles; Allah created these for the creatures to live on and in the earth. He knows all things and sends winds that raise the clouds.

Under the sky, Allah spread the clouds according to his will, and he broke the clouds into fragments until the creatures saw rain. He sent down a rain of water and created fruits of varying types and colors. Allah created the mountains, which have varying colors, like white and red mountains. And Allah created jinn (unseen creatures), such as Satan (evil), from nonflammable fire and created the angels from light.

Who did create Allah, the creator of the universe?

[Say, He is Allah, the one only; Allah, the Eternal Absolute; He begets not, nor is He begotten; And there is none like unto him (The Quran Translation, Ali, Yusuf 2007, 112:1–4)].

[Allah! there is no God but He, the living, the self-sustaining, Eternal. No slumber can seize Him nor sleep. His are all things in the heavens and on earth (The Quran Translation, Ali, Yusuf 2007, 2:255)].

No one created Allah. No one is related to Allah. He has no begotten sons. He has no begotten daughters, and there is no anyone similar to him. Allah, the creator of the universe is an absolute one. He does not deliver. He was not born.

The First Human (Adam)

The story of Adam according to the interpretation of Islamic resources, Allah, the creator of the universe, informed the angels that he would create the first human to live on the earth.

The angels asked Allah, "Majesty, do you place a human, who will cause disruption and drips blood, on the earth, while we worship you and glorify you?"

According to interpretations of the Islamic resources, the reply of Allah denoted that Allah has all the knowledge and they do not recognize. Allah created the first man, Adam, from the dust of clay. And Allah blew a soul into Adam. All the angels and Iblis (evil) from unseen jinn, got a command from Allah to prostrate themselves before Adam. All the Angels prostrated themselves to Adam except Iblis (evil), who refused to obey the command of Allah.

[Behold! your Lord said to the angels: I am about to create man, from sounding clay from mud molded into shape; When I have fashioned him (in due proportion) and breathed into him: of My spirit, fall you down in obeisance unto him. So, the angels prostrated themselves, all of them together: Not so Iblis: he refused to be among those: who prostrated themselves (The Quran Translation, Ali, Yusuf 2007, 15:28–50)].

Iblis (Satan) was questioned by Allah about what was prevented him from prostrating himself to the first human, Adam? Iblis was arrogant; did Iblis think that he was one of the chief angels? Iblis rejected faith and replied, "I am better than Adam. You, Allah, created me from nonflammable fire and created Adam from the clay of dust."

Allah's command to Iblis (evil) was: to get out of the garden. Iblis was accursed, and the curse got him from that time to the Day of Resurrection.

"Allah, give me delay until the Day of Resurrection," Iblis asked Allah. The delay was permitted to the appointed time of the Day of Resurrection. And Iblis (evil) said, "Allah has put me with sinners. I will make defiance gorgeous to Adam and his offspring, and I will mislead them. I promise you that I will put them all with the sinners except your sincere servants, who are purified by your grace."

In the interpretation of Islamic resources, Allah's decision denoted that Iblis, and all his followers will live in the fire of hell forever. Allah taught names (titles) to Adam and questioned the angels to tell him all the names if they knew.

The angels said, "Gratefulness to Allah; we have no knowledge except what you have taught us. You Allah has all the knowledge and wisdom."

Adam obeyed Allah and said to the angels all their names. Allah knew what the angels did not know. Allah created a wife to Adam and permitted them to live in the eternal garden and don't eat from the forbidden tree.

Iblis (evil) whispered ideas to Adam and his wife to bring their shame that was hidden from their vision. Iblis said to Adam and his wife, "if you eat from the forbidden tree, you both will live forever. I promise both of you. I am to you an honest adviser." Iblis trapped Adam and his wife in his deceptions. And when they ate the fruits of the forbidden tree, they felt unwell. Iblis shredded their clothes to expose their bodies. They cut from the leaves of the trees to cover themselves. Adam and his wife had received words from Allah that they should not eat from the forbidden tree, and Iblis (evil) was an actual enemy to both.

"We are wrongdoers, and if Allah does not forgive us and grant us mercy, we will be among the losers," Adam and his wife said.

Adam, his wife, and Iblis got an order from Allah to descend from the garden because Adam and his wife followed Iblis (evil). The earth was a place for their settlement and gratification. On the earth, they lived, and they died, and on the Day of Resurrection, they will come up from the earth.

Adam received blessed holy words from Allah. Adam became the first prophet. Adam and his wife repented. Allah forgave them, Allah is the forgiver, and he is the most gracious and merciful. To Allah, the creator of the universe, belongs the higher power. Allah is the only divine, and there is no other divine.

Adam's Sons

The story of Adam's sons is according to the interpretation of Islamic resources. In three stages of darkness, Allah, the creator of the universe, created the human in the mother's abdomen, uterus. Allah granted the children of Adam resources to have clothes to cover their bodies and for beautification, although, the cover of deep faith is better. Allah created eight heads of cattle in pairs.

[O you children of Adam! Let not Satan seduce you, in the same manner as he got your parents out of the Garden, stripping them of their raiment to expose their shame: for he and his tribe watch you from a position where you cannot see them: We made the Evil one's friends (only) to those without faith (The Quran Translation, Ali, Yusuf 2007, 7:26-35)].

In the interpretation of Islamic resources, the children of Adam got instructions from Allah that they should not let the evil (Iblis) deceive them such as he deceived their father and mother. Evil and his groups see people from location they could not see. The evil groups are friends to those unbelievers.

Adam's two sons sacrificed food. Allah accepted the sacrifice from one of them and did not accept it from the other one. Adam's son felt sad because his sacrifice was unacceptable.

The blessed son told his brother, "Allah accepts sacrifice from faithful believers."

The sinner brother got angry, and he wanted to kill his blessed brother.

Adam's blessed son said to his sinner brother, "if you extend your hand to murder me, I am not extending my hand to murder you. You will earn my sins and your sins. You will go the hellfire that is the punishment of transgressors."

Adam's wicked son killed his blessed brother and became offender. This was the first crime done by a human in the world. Then, he watched a bird that buried the body of another bird in the ground. He said, "I did not bury my brother's body in the graveyard. I missed being like the bird who buried the body of another bird." He felt guilty.

According to the interpretation of Islamic resources, Allah sent to Moses the Torah for the children of Israel which denoted, if one killed a soul of a human without a soul of a human or exploitation in the earth, as if he killed all the humans. And if one kept the life of a soul of a human, as if he kept the life of all the humans.

CHAPTER 3

The Messengers and Prophets

THIS BOOK INCLUDES THE STORIES OF MESSENGERS, PROPHETS OF ALLAH, the creator of the universe, according to interpretation of Islamic resources: Noah (Nuh), Enoch (Idris), Salish (Saleh), Hud (Houd), Abraham (Ibrahim), Ishmael (Ismail), Lot (Lut), Jonah (Yunes), Jacob (Yaqub), Isaac (Isehaq), Joseph (Yusuf), Shuaib, Moses (Musa), Aron (Haroun), Talut (Saul), King David (Dawoud), Solomon (Suleiman), Ezra (Uzair), Amran (Imran), Zacharias (Zakariya), John the Baptist (Yahya), Jesus (Isa) and Muhamad (Ahmad), and the men of truth are: the Wise Luqman, King Zul-qarnain, the Companions of the Cave, Job (Ayyub). They invited the people of their nations to believe while the people were against them, peace is on them all.

Those prophets, messengers and the men of truth worshipped Allah, the creator of the universe, and they did not associate with him. They overcame distress, and they fulfilled good deeds and obeyed Allah's commands. The angel Gabriel (Jabril) brought the Arabic Holy Quran from Allah, the creator of universe to the prophet and messenger Muhamad over twenty-three years. The Arabic Holy Quran has 114 chapters (*surah*) and includes the stories of prophets and messengers of Allah. The author wrote these stories according to the interpretation of Islamic resources.

The translation of Arabic holy Quran to English, which are in the markets, might not be accurate. The objectives of writing of these stories are to let the readers to know the Islamic point of view and to introduce the similarities and differences of the heavenly religions. These stories include clarification of the real situations that happened in the past centuries to offer the readers valid information. Every story is as it is. And there is no obligation of religion; the reader has freedom of choice.

The Messenger Noah (Nuh)

The synopsis of the story of the prophet Noah (Nuh) is according to the interpretation of Islamic resources. Allah, the creator of the universe, sent the prophet and messenger Noah (Nuh) on a mission. Noah advised the people to worship Allah, the creator of the heavens, earth, and everything in between. Noah said to his people, "I come to you with signs that you should worship Allah. I fear for you the torment of the Day of Resurrection."

[We sent Noah to his people, (with the command): Warn your People before there comes to them a grievous penalty (The Quran Translation, Ali, Yusuf 2007, 71:1-28)].

The unbelievers made fun of Noah (Nuh), and they continued in their entertainment. They also worshipped statues and refused to listen to him. He continued to advise them.

"We see you nothing, but a man like ourselves, And we see that those who follow you are the meanest among us; they are silly. We do not see in you any worth above us. We think that you and your followers are liars," the rejecters said to Noah.

The prophet Noah (Nuh) said, "My people, I have a sign from Allah that he has sent compassion to me. His mercy was hidden from your sight. We will not obligate people to believe the truth when they are against it. My nation's people, I do not want your recompense; my recompense is from Allah. I will not ignore those who believe, and I see that you are unknowing. My people, who will save me from the punishment if I ignore the believers? Do you not have minds? I did not say that I have treasures, nor that I know what is hidden, nor did I claim to be a chief angel. Nor did I say that those people who are disgusting in your eyes will not be granted rewards. Allah knows how they think. If I do what you want, I will be with sinners."

"Noah, you prolonged the arguing with us. Now, bring what you threaten us if you speak the truth," the rejecters said.

The rejecters went to worship the statues that they had made by their hands. Noah stayed, inviting them 950 years, but there was no way. "I would like to give you advice: Allah will bring punishment to you if he wills it, and you will not be able to overcome it. Allah is your creator, and to him, you will return," Noah said. "If you do not shut up, we will stone you to death," the people said, threatening Noah. After 950 years of advising, the prophet Noah (Nuh) cried and asked Allah to help him. According to the interpretation of Islamic resources, Allah informed Noah (Nuh) that there would not be any more believers except those who believed. And Noah should not have sorrow over their evil work. And Allah commanded Noah (Nuh) to build an ark (ship) and said that Noah should not address those who were sinners again. They were about to be devastated by flood.

Noah (Nuh) built the ark (ship), and every time the unbelievers passed by him, they made fun of him. "If you are laughing now, we will laugh soon, and you will know who will have a penalty that will cover them with humiliation," Noah said.

Allah's command came. The water poured out from the fountains of the earth. This was a sign to Noah (Nuh) to go on board. He boarded two couples of each kind of creatures onto the ship—two males and two females—along with his family and the few people who believed him.

"In the name of Allah, the creator of the universe, start boarding the ship, whether moving or at rest. Allah is the forgiver and the most generous," Noah said to the believers. Then Noah said to his son, "come here for boarding with us, and do not stay with the sinners."

"I will take myself to a cave on a mountain; it will save me from the flood waters," Noah's son replied.

"This day, nothing can be saved from the command of Allah except those who are on this ship. They are safe by Allah's mercy," Noah (Nuh) said to his son. His son had separated from the rest of the people and refused to go.

"Allah, your promise is real. You exist and are the honor judge of Justice. Save my son," the prophet Noah (Nuh) said.

Allah informed Noah (Nuh) that Noah's son was not upright, and he was not moral. The prophet Noah received advice that he should not be ignorant. He should not request for what he did not realize. "Allah, I ask your protection, because I asked you for something I did not know. I will go astray without your guidance. Forgive me, and grant me mercy, amen," Noah prayed to Allah.

Noah's wife had deceived him. Noah's wife and his son were included with the sinners who were drowned by the floods. The ark (ship) moved on high waves like mountains. The command of Allah, the creator of the universe, was accomplished. The flood came, and the land was flooded out. As the waves came between them, Noah's son was among those who were drowned in the flood. According to the interpretation of Islamic resources, Allah's commands is as follows: the earth was to swallow the water, the sky was to withhold the rains, the water was to recede, and the matter was ended. The unbelievers, who were against Allah's words, vanished. Noah's ark rested on a mountain's beach away from those sinners. The prophet Noah received instructions to come out from the ship with peace and blessing. Few people moved with Noah. If those people went astray, Allah gave them pleasure for a while in their lives. On the Day of Resurrection, a penalty will reach the transgressors.

The Messenger Enoch (Idris)

The synopsis of the story of the messenger and prophet Enoch (Idris), (peace on him) is according to the Islamic resources. The prophet Enoch (Idris) was a messenger and a prophet of Allah, the creator of the universe. The prophet Enoch (Idris) invited the ancient Egyptians and many people around the world to worship Allah, the creator of the universe, and did not associate with him. And the prophet Enoch invited the people to believe in the Day of Resurrection and to use wisdom. He told them to worship and ask Allah directly, without mediators (communion). He taught them to write on papyrus and taught them the value of wisdom. The prophet Enoch (Idris) said, "all the people were equal. No one was better than others, except if he or she had the deep faith in Allah, the creator of the universe." The pharaoh and the ancient Egyptians were arrogant. They worshipped other things, such as the Nile River, the sun, cats, statues, snakes, cows, and pharaohs. They refused to believe the prophet and messenger Enoch (Idris), and they decided to kill him.

[Also mention in the book: the case of Idris: he was a man of truth (and sincerity), (and) a prophet: And We raised to a lofty station (The Quran Translation, Ali, Yusuf 2007, 19:56-57)].

Allah, the creator of the universe, saved Enoch (Idris) and raised him to the heavens. Then, the prophet Enoch (Idris) died naturally. The soul of the prophet Enoch (Idris) lives with other prophets and messengers in the heavenly eternal garden.

The prophet Hud (Houd)

The synopsis of the story of the prophet Hud (Houd) is according to the interpretation of Islamic resources. The prophet and messenger Hud (Houd) said, "Aad people, you should worship Allah, the creator of the universe. I do not ask you for compensation. I will have a reward from Allah. Allah created me and all of you."

[To the Aad People (We sent) Hud, one their own brothers. He said: "O my people worship Allah, you have no other god but Him." (The Quran Translation, Ali, Yusuf 2007, 11:50–60)].

"Hud, you did not come by signs. We will not leave the statues of our gods that we worship. We will not follow you. Our gods' images will hurt you," the people of Aad said.

"Allah is my witness, and you are witness that I do not associate with Allah. I depend on him, and there is no creature out of his hand. He is on the straight way. My people of Aad, ask for forgiveness and repent. He will send rain and increase your strength. You have no other divine; you are transgressors. Will you not fear Allah?" the prophet Hud (Houd) said.

"We perceive that you have religious madness, and we believe that you are a deceiver," the leader of the rejecters replied.

"My people, there is no madness in me, but I am a prophet and messenger. I tell you messages of Allah, and I am an honest adviser to you. Allah created the seven heavens, earth, and everything natural in between. Are you astonished that a prophet and messenger came to remind you? Are you astonished that advice was given through a man from your tribe? Remember that Allah made you successors after the people of Noah and increased your heights. Remember the grace of Allah to you is that you are wealthy," the prophet Hud said.

"Do you want us to worship your God alone and leave the statues of our gods? Our fathers used to worship these statues. Bring whatever you have threatened us. if you are telling the truth," the rejecters of Aad said.

"My people, ask forgiveness of Allah and repent to him. Allah will send from the sky plenty of rain and will add strength to your strength. Do not turn away, as the unbelievers did," Hud said. "You did not bring us visible signs. We will not leave our gods' statues, which we worship. And we do not believe you," Aad people said. "You associate partners with Allah, the creator of the universe. So, arrange your worst plan against me, and do not give me relief. I put my trust in Allah, the creator of heavens, earth, and every natural thing in between. Allah grasps all creatures' souls, and he is on the straight path. If you turn away, I have told you the message honestly. He will create other people after you. Allah has the higher power, and he watches all things," the prophet Hud (Houd) said.

"We will not talk anymore, but our gods' statues will harm you with a curse," the unbelievers of Aad said.

"You are arguing with me over names that you and your fathers have called without Allah's permission, fury and anger have already fallen on you. I am among those who are waiting," Hud said. Allah's command was issued. Allah saved the prophet Hud (Houd) and those who believed from serious penalty. The Aad people rejected the proof, refused to believe. And they defied the prophet messenger Hud (Houd). They followed the orders of their arrogant, stubborn tyrant leaders, and they got a punishment on their lives. On the Day of Resurrection, they will go the hell. Allah cut the origins of those who rejected his signs and rejected his words.

The prophet Salish (Saleh)

The synopsis of the story of the prophet Salish (Saleh) is according to the interpretation of Islamic resources. To Thamud people, their brother Salish (Saleh) said, "my people, worship the creator of the heavens, earth, and everything in between. There is no other divine. He created you from the clay of dust and granted you, waterfall, harvest parks, and palm trees. And you built houses on the mountains, and you brought rocks to shape in the valley. Ask forgiveness and repent. He is near and listening," Salish (Saleh) said.

"You have lived among us as a good man. We wished that you would become our leader until this new matter, which you said. You want us to leave our gods' statues and worship your Allah. You want us to prohibit worshipping of our gods' statues, which our forefathers worshipped. We distrust your invitation. Why do you want us to worship an absolute one God?" Thamud people said.

"Will you not fear Allah, the creator of the universe? Will you not submit your faith to him? I am a prophet messenger to you. Fear Allah and save the message of absolute oneness and follow me. I do not ask you for recompense; my recompense is only from Allah; He created humankind and unseen creatures, such as jinn and angels. Allah created the heavens, earth, and everything in between," Salish (Saleh) said. The leaders of Thamud people denied the upcoming Day of Resurrection and said, "Salish (Saleh) is no more than a human, like us. He eats as we eat, and he drinks such as we drink. If we obey a human like us, we will vanish. He promised us that when we will die, when we decay, we will be awakened to life. His promise is false. There is only one life that we live, and we will not be resurrected. He is just a human who invents lies against the statues of our gods that we worship. We must not believe him."

"Thamud people, do not follow the order of your leaders, who are unbelievers, offenders, and sinners. They make disruption in the land," the prophet Salish (Saleh) said.

"You are witch, and you are human like us. Show us a sign if you are prophet of God," the Thamud people replied.

[To the Thamud people: (We sent) Salish, one of their own brothers: He said: "O my people, worship Allah; you have no other god but Him. Now has come to you a clear (Sign) from your Lord! This she-camel of Allah is a Sign unto you: so, leave her to graze in Allah's earth, and let her come to no harm, or you shall be seized with a grievous punishment" (The Quran Translation, Ali, Yusuf 2007, 7:73-79)].

"My people, I have evidence of my message from Allah. Here is a female camel. She is a clear sign to you. Leave her to eat in the land. The camel has the right to drink water, as you do. Plan a time for her to drink water. Do not touch her with any abuse and fear that a penalty will take you away. Who can help me against Allah if I defy him?" Salish (Saleh) said.

Thamud people became two divisions: parties—believers and unbelievers—who contradicted each other. The unbelievers killed the female camel, and they became sinners. "Allah, the creator of the universe, help me because Thamud people deny my message," the prophet Salish (Saleh) prayed. In the interpretation of Islamic resources, Allah informed the prophet Salish (Saleh) that in a little while, they would be punished.

"Stay in your homes just three days; there will be a threat that cannot be resisted," the prophet Salish (Saleh) warned the Thamud people again. Nine families caused exploitation on the earth. They planned to kill the prophet and Salish (Saleh) and his family at night, and they arranged to deny their acts. Allah's plan came before their plan. Allah saved the prophet Salish (Saleh) and the believers who were faithful. The punishment overtook the rejecters as a strong earthquake. They vanished with the people who were sinners before them. They did not anticipate their punishment, and they could not delay it. And Allah sent messengers in succession with justice. Every time the rejecters said, "the prophets and messengers are liars," Allah punished the unbelievers because they followed each other. Thamud people vanished because they did not believe. Allah, the creator of the universe, has the higher power. And Allah created other generations.

Job (Ayyub)

The synopsis of the story of Job (Ayyub) is according to the interpretation of Islamic resources. Job (Ayyub) was a man of truth; he lost his wealth and his children while he had a painful illness. All his friends and his family left him except his wife, and he had countless patience.

[Commemorate Our Servant Job. Behold he cried to his lord: "the evil One has affected me with distress and suffering!" (The Command was given): "Strike with your foot: here is (water) wherein to wash, cool and (water) to drink" (The Quran Translation, Ali, Yusuf 2007, 38:41–45)].

Job (Ayyub) cried and prayed to Allah, the creator of the universe, during the time of his painful suffering and said, "please, Allah, heal and cure me. Satan harmed me with illness."

According to the interpretation of Islamic resources, Allah, the creator of the universe, inspired to Job (Ayyub) to drink water from a spring, insert his leg in the cold spring water, and put a little mud on his skin lesions.

And Allah healed Job (Ayyub) and bring back his family and gave him similar number of children. One day, Job's wife came late. Allah inspired to Job (Ayyub) to take a small bunch of grass and to beat his wife gently because he swore in the name of Allah to beat her. So, people should not swear by Allah in vain and should not say false oaths.

The Companions of the Cave

The story of the Companions of the Cave is according to the interpretation of Islamic resources. A group of young men escaped to a cave to save themselves from the people of their nation. They believed in Allah, the creator of the universe, and they were men of truth. The people of their nation refused to believe, and they wanted to kill the young men.

[Or do you reflect that the companions of the cave and of inscription were wonders among our signs? Behold, The youths betook themselves to the cave: they said, "Our Lord bestow on us Mercy from Yourself, and dispose of our affair for us in the right way!" (The Quran Translation, Ali, Yusuf 2007, 18:9-31)].

The companions of the cave said, "we believe in Allah, and we will never associate with him. We will pray to Allah to guide us." According to the interpretation of Islamic resources, Allah's miracle happened: the companions of the cave slept for hundreds of years. No one knew that they were sleeping; those who saw them thought they were wakeful and got scared. And their dog extended his arms at the entrance of the cave. And Allah sent angels to turn them on their right side and on their left side. The sun rose on their right sides, and the sun set on their left sides. One day, Allah allowed the young men to wake up.

They asked each other, "how long did we nap?"

"We might have slept for a day or a few days," they said to each other. They told one of them to take their money and go to buy food and to be nice with people. If their nation found them, they might force them to share others' beliefs or to stone them to death. The villagers knew that the companions of the cave had money papers from the past centuries. They found the companions in the cave. The villagers became believers. Allah, the creator of the universe, made this miracle happen for those young men. After that, when the companions of the cave died, the villagers built a temple above the cave.

This story proves the upcoming Day of Resurrection. And the individual should not say that he or she will do anything tomorrow, but should say, "I shall do it, as Allah wills."

King Zul-qarnain

The summary of the story of the king Zul-qarnain is according to the interpretation of Islamic resources. Zul-qarnain was a man of truth, and he was guided by Allah.

[They ask you concerning Zul-qarnain. Say, "I will rehearse to you something of his story." "Verily We established his power on the earth, and We gave him the ways and the means to all ends" (The Quran Translation, Ali, Yusuf 2007, 18:83-104)].

Allah, the creator of the universe, granted Zul-qarnain authority and establishment on the earth. Zul-qarnain went to the west of the earth, where he found transgressors.

King Zul-qarnain said, "the criminals will be punished, and they will have another punishment after life, by the promise of Allah. Those who accomplish upright deeds will have the promised rewards of the eternal garden."

King Zul-qarnain went to the east of the earth; he found people who did not know anything. They did not know how to protect themselves from the sun. While he was moving between two mountains; he found people who asked him to protect them from

Gog (Yagog) and Mog (Magog) because they caused exploitations on the earth.

King Zul-qarnain said, "let me build a strong barrier wall between you all and Gog (Yagog) and Mog (Magog). They cannot penetrate it, except if Allah wills."

Allah, the creator of the universe, sent information to King Zul-qarnain that the barrier would stay intact until the signs that would appear before the Day of Resurrection. Zul-qarnain said, "you all help me. Give me melted steel, and blow on it until it become red. Then put melted copper on it to build the barrier wall."

They helped King Zul-qarnain to build the barrier wall between the two mountains, and it is still intact now. It will be destroyed as a sign before the Day of Resurrection. And Gog (Yagog) and Mog (Magog) will cause corruption on the earth again. This is the promise of Allah, and the promise of Allah is the truth.

The `Messenger Abraham (Ibrahim)

The story of the prophet Ibrahim, or Abraham (peace on him), is according to the interpretation of Islamic resources. Abraham was born in a famous ancient city called Babel, Iraq. The people worshipped statues and stars there, but the prophet Abraham (Ibrahim) refused to worship these things. At night, the prophet Abraham looked at the sky. He watched the stars, and he watched the moon rising in brilliance. Abraham said, "this is not the creator of the universe." In the morning, the prophet Abraham watched the sunrise, and in the evening, he watched the sunset. The sun and the stars disappeared.

The prophet Abraham said, "these things are not Allah, the creator of the universe. My people, I am free from your lies of associating with Allah. The real creator of the universe never vanishes. If Allah does not guide me, I will go off track."

The Signs of Allah

The prophet Abraham recognized that Allah, the creator of the universe saw him, but Abraham could not see Allah. Allah showed Abraham the power and the rules of the heavens and the earth to give him an assured understanding. Ibrahim followed the prophet Noah's way, and he kept the virtuous honest.

[Behold! Abraham said: "My Lord: Show me how You give life to the dead." He said: "Do you not yet believe?" Yes (I believe)! But to satisfy my own understanding." He said: "Take four birds; tame them to turn to you; put a portion of them on every hill, call to them: they will come to you (flying) with speed. Then know that Allah is Exalted in Power, Wise" (The Quran Translation, Ali, Yusuf 2007, 2:260)].

Abraham said, "please, Allah, show me—how do you resurrect the deceased?"

According to the interpretation of Islamic resources, Allah questioned the prophet Abraham (Ibrahim): "Would you not have faith in Allah?"

Abraham said, "Allah, I have faith in you, but I just wanted to reassure my heart."

The prophet Abraham received an order from Allah to kill four birds, to cut them into pieces, and to put their pieces on the mountains. Then, Abraham should call them in the name of Allah, and they should come back to him, flying quickly. The prophet Abraham obeyed. The birds were resurrected to life and came back to Abraham flying quickly.

The prophet Abraham (Ibrahim) said, "Allah is the greatest and wisest. I will never worship partners with Allah. I submit my faith to Allah. Allah created the seven heavens, earth, and everything in between."

After a time, Allah granted the wisdom and the message to Abraham (Ibrahim). The prophet Abraham said to his father, Azur, "why do you worship statues? I see you and your people going astray."

The prophet Abraham said to the people of Babel, "What are these statues to which you are loyal to them?"

"We found our fathers worshipping them," the people of Babel said.

"You and your fathers are committing visible sins," the prophet Abraham said.

"Are you speaking the truth or are you joking?" the people of Babel asked.

The prophet Abraham said to the leader of Babel, "let us debate the religion of Allah. He has guided me. I do not fear your statues that you worship. Nothing can happen to me except by Allah's will. He knows all things. How can I fear the statues while you associate with Allah, the creator of the universe? You associate with him without any permission. Who provides more security?"

The prophet Abraham (Ibrahim) said to the leader of Babel, "Allah, the creator of the universe, has the higher power. Allah does not guide transgressors. He is the creator of the heavens, earth, and everything in between. He has created you, and I am a witness to his power. I do not follow you, and I do not associate with him. I reject your belief. And I have opposition and animosity with you all until you believe. I worship Allah only."

[Have you not turned your vision to one who disputed with Abraham about his Lord, because Allah has granted him power? Abraham said: "My Lord is He Who gives life and death." He said: "I give life and death." Said Abraham: "But He is Allah that causes the sun to rise from the East: do you then cause it to rise from the West." thus was confounded who in arrogance rejected faith. Nor does Allah give guidance to a people unjust (The Quran Translation, Ali, Yusuf 2007, 2:258)].

"Allah provides life and causes death," the prophet Abraham said.

"I provide life and cause death," the leader of babel said arrogantly.

"Allah created the sun and ordered it to rise from east. Can you make the sun rise from the west?" Abraham asked the leader of Babel.

The leader of Babel was impressed and stopped. Abraham was

letting the leader of babel knew that he was a human and could not control the universe.

[Also mention in the Book (the story of) Abraham he was a man of Truth, a prophet. Behold, he said to his father: "O my father! Why you worship that which does not hear and does not see, and can profit you nothing? O my father! To me has come knowledge: which has not reached you: so, follow me: I will guide you to a way that is even and straight" (The Quran Translation, Ali, Yusuf 2007, 19:41-50)].

Abraham said to his father, Azur, "Allah is the creator of the universe. I trust him. I turn in repentance to him, and my final goal is to Allah. Please, Allah, forgive the believers and guide my father, amen. What are those that you worship? You worship a false god. What is your knowledge of Allah? I will pray to Allah to forgive you, although I do not have permission on your behalf."

Abraham said to the people of Babel in the temple, "I get sick of your ignorance. And I promise that I will have a plan for your statues after you go away."

After the people of Babel went out of the temple, Abraham turned to the statues, which the people worshipped, and said, "will not you eat the food that was offered to you? What is the matter with you? Why do you not talk?" The prophet Abraham turned on the statues and hit them with his right hand. He crushed them to pieces, except the huge statue because the people of Babel would return to the temple, and Abraham would talk to them. In Babel, the worshippers of the statues rushed back to the temple and asked, "who destroyed the statues of our gods?"

"We heard a young man was talking to them and rejecting them. He is called Abraham (Ibrahim)," someone said.

The leaders and chiefs of Babel asked their servants to bring Abraham, in front of the people; they would be witnesses.

The leaders of Babel asked Abraham, "did you destroy the statues of our gods that we worship?"

"No, the largest statue broke them all. Ask him if he can talk to you," Abraham said.

The people of Babel got angry with the prophet Abraham and said, "you know well that these statues do not talk."

"Do you worship statues that you have made by your hands? Allah has created you and your handiwork," Abraham said.

"Abraham, you are the one who broke our statues," they said.

"Do you take partners with Allah that cannot help you or damage you? Shame on you and upon the things you worship. Those images cannot help you. Do you not have wisdom? You should worship Allah, the creator of the universe, and fear him so that he may forgive you if you understand. Now, you worship statues, and you formulate lies. The statues which you worship do not have the power to give you food. Ask Allah to give you food. You should serve him and be thankful to him. You will return to him. And if you reject the message, remember that generations before you did that, and they vanished," Abraham said.

"The messenger and prophets have the right to speak freely and openly. Allah creates all the creatures. Allah replaces them; it is easy for Allah. If you want to know how Allah created the world, you can go around the earth and watch. Allah has all the higher power over the universe. He punishes whomever he wants, and he grants mercy to whomever he wants. You all will return to him. No one on the earth or in the heavens will be able to flee from Allah's plan. No one can have a protector or helper without his permission. Those who reject Allah's signs and deny the Day of Resurrection, will suffer a grievous penalty," the prophet Abraham said.

"Kill Abraham (Ibrahim) or burn him," the leaders and the people of Babel said.

"You all associate partners with Allah, the creator of the universe? Now, you have love and admiration between yourselves, but on the Day of Resurrection, you all will have conflicts with yourselves, and you all will curse yourselves. Your place will be the fire of hell, and you will not have any help," the prophet Abraham (Ibrahim) said to the people of Babel.

"Burn Abraham and keep the nobility of our gods' statues. Build a big oven for him, and throw him into the fire," the leaders of Babel said. The people of Babel conspired against the prophet Abraham, but Allah made them losers. According to the interpretation of Islamic resources, Allah commanded the fire to be cold and peaceful on Abraham (Ibrahim). And Allah humiliated the unbelievers. Allah saved Abraham (Ibrahim) and the prophet Lot (Lut), his nephew, and directed them to a holy land, which was blessed for the nations. The prophet Abraham said, "Allah will guide me to the straight way. I have submitted my faith to Allah, the creator of the universe."

The Prophet Ishmael (Ismail)

The story of the prophet and messenger Ishmael (Ismail) is according to the Islamic resources. The prophet Abraham (Ibrahim) married a young lady from Egypt (Messer) called Hagar because his first wife, Sarah, was barren. The prophet Abraham (Ibrahim) prayed to Allah, the creator of the universe, "grant me serenity and a blessed son."

Allah granted Abraham (Ibrahim) a son from Hagar called Ishmael (Ismail). The prophet Abraham left his wife, Hagar, and his son, Ismail, in a valley that had no plants, called Makah in Hijaz, Saudi Arabia.

[O our Lord! I have made some of my offspring to dwell in a valley without cultivation, by your Sacred House; in order, that they may establish regular Prayer; so, fill the hearts of some among men with love toward them, and feed them with fruits: so that they may give thanks (The Quran Translation, Ali, Yusuf 2007, 14:37)].

The water in the valley of Makah was finished. The infant Ishmael (Ismail) cried from thirst while his mother, Hagar, carried him. She ran between the two mountains, Al-Safa, and Al-Marwa, and prayed, "Allah, will you please, grant my son water to drink, he is crying and dehydrated?" The miracle of Allah happened, and a huge waterfall of Zamzam opened. It is there to this day.

Allah sent to the prophet Abraham (Ibrahim) a holy book, such as he sent holy book to the prophet Moses (Musa) who was one of

Abraham's descendants. Then Abraham went on mission of trips to invite the tribes to believe in Allah. The prophet Abraham's prayer was, "Please Allah, make Makah a safe village, grant crops to its people and prevent us from worshipping statues. The images of the statues have confused people. Those who follow my ways are like me. You are the most merciful. Please give grace to those who believe and forgive them on the Day of Resurrection."

Allah, the creator of the universe, granted the prophet Abraham (Ibrahim) his requests. Even Allah gives the unbelievers gratification for a while. Then, he will send the unbelievers to a painful punishment of hellfire.

Abraham's (Ibrahim's) Dream

While Ismail was a youth, the prophet Abraham (Ibrahim) said to Ishmael (Ismail), "my son, in a vision of dream I saw that I offered you as a slaughtered sacrifice to Allah. Now, what is your opinion?" "My father, obey the command of Allah. You will find me one of those who has patience," the prophet Ishmael (Ismail) said.

[So, when they had both submitted their wills (to Allah), and he had laid him prostrate on his forehead (for sacrifice), We called out to him, "O Abraham! You have already fulfilled the vision!" thus indeed do We reward those who do right. For this was obviously trial And We ransomed him with momentous sacrifice (The Quran Translation, Ali, Yusuf 2007, 37:103-109)].

Both Abraham and Ishmael (Ismail) had deep faith in Allah. Abraham got Ishmael (Ismail) to prostrate on his forehead, ready for sacrifice. Before the prophet Abraham put the knife on Ismael's neck, Allah inspired to Abraham that he fulfilled the vision of dream and Allah sent a large sheep to Abraham (Ibrahim) to slaughter for sacrifice. Allah saved the life of Ishmael (Ismail). This had been a trial. They both behaved righteously and were obedient. After Abraham passed the trial and achieved the command, Allah rewarded the prophet Abraham (Ibrahim) and made him a messenger prophet for all the nations of the worlds.

"What about my offspring?" Abraham asked Allah.

According to the interpretation of Islamic resources, the promise of mercy of Allah did not include the transgressors. And Allah ordered Abraham and his son Ismail to build the sacred house of Makah (Al-Kabbah). Allah blessed the sacred house in Makah as a safe place for people. He ordered the prophet Ibrahim and Ismail to clean the sacred mosque at Makah for those who walked around and for those who stayed for worshipping, praying, and bending and kneeling to Allah—those who did not associate anything in worshipping Allah. The believers should pray in the corner of the prophet Abraham (Ibrahim). Anyone who rejected the religion of the prophet Abraham (Ibrahim) harmed himself.

The prophet Abraham (Ibrahim) was the father of prophet, messengers, and he will be on the Day of Resurrection with the honored, virtuous people. The prophet Abraham (Ibrahim) prayed while he was carrying the foundations of the first sacred house (Al-Kabbah) with Ishmael (Ismail): "praise is to Allah, please accept our work. Keep us believers by submission of our faith to you, and from our offspring make a population of believers. Show us the worthy faith, accept our repentance, and forgive us. You listen and have all knowledge. Allah is merciful and forgiving. Will you please, Allah, send among the believers of Makah a messenger from them, who will read to them your holy book, teach them wisdom, and purify them. You are wise."

The Guests of the Prophet Abraham (Ibrahim)

"Peace is on you," the angels said.

"Peace is on you all," Abraham said. He thought, *Those people appear unfamiliar.* He entered the kitchen of his family, bringing a huge, cooked calf, and placed it in front of the angels. "Why do you not eat?" he asked.

When they did not eat, Abraham saw that their upper limbs were different from human upper limbs; they were shorter. He got frightened of them, and said, "I'm afraid of you men."

"Do not be afraid. We are angels, messengers of Allah, the creator of the universe, and we came to tell you glad news. You will have a blessed son—his name is Isaac (Isehaq)—and a grandson; his name is Jacob (Yaqub)."

Abraham's wife, Sarah laughed. She hit her face and said, "Oh Allah, I will deliver a son while I am a barren old woman, and my husband is an old man. This is an astonishing thing." The angels said, "are you astonished by the mercy of Allah? Peace be upon you all, the people of this blessed house. He has decided, and he is the wisest and has all the knowledge." Good news came from Allah to the prophet Abraham (Ibrahim) that he would have a son called Isaac (Isehaq) and a grandson called Jacob (Yaqub). They were faithful, and Allah blessed them.

[Abraham said: What then is the business that on which you (have come), O you messengers (of Allah)? They said: "We have been sent to a people (deep) in sin, Expecting the adherent of Lut: we are certainly (charged) to save them (from harm), all except his wife, who we have ascertained, will be among those who will lag behind" (The Quran Translation, Ali, Yusuf 2007, 15: 57-75)].

Abraham asked the angels, "what is your mission here?" According to the interpretation of Islamic resources, the angels said, "Allah commanded us to go to villagers of serious sins. They approached men (they used same-sex relationships)."

"Lot (Lut), my nephew, is living there," Abraham said.

"We know who is living there. We will save him and the believers, except his wife. She was one of the sinners. She deceived Lot (Lut)," the angels said.

According to the interpretation of Islamic resources, the angels fulfilled and accomplished the command of Allah, the creator of the universe, and a shower of hot baked clay such as rocks had fallen down to kill those transgressors. They invaded the boundaries. First, They saved the believers who were there, but they did not find any believers, except in one house. And they placed a sign for people to fear the grievous penalty. In the interpretation of Islamic resources, Allah granted Abraham (Ibrahim) a second son, called Isaac (Isehaq), and a grandson, called Jacob (Yaqub). And Allah ordered the messages and sacred scriptures among the offspring of Abraham. Allah rewarded Abraham (Ibrahim) during his life, and Abraham will be with the companion of messengers in paradise, on the Day of Resurrection.

Abraham was not Jewish or Christian, but he was a man of reality, and he submitted his faith to Allah, the creator of the universe. He did not associate partners with Allah. That was the law that he left to his offspring.

[And this was the legacy that Abraham left to his sons, and so did Jacob; "Oh my sons! Allah has chosen the Faith for you; not except in the Faith of Islam" (The Quran Translation, Ali, Yusuf 2007, 2:132-133)].

Abraham said to his offspring before his death, "my children, before you all die, be sure that you submit your faith to Allah, the creator of the universe. Allah has chosen the righteous for you. He knows everything that we hid, and he knows everything that we reveal. There is no hidden issue from Allah, whether on earth or in the heavens. I praise Allah: He granted me two sons, Ismail (Ishmael) and Isaac (Isehaq) in my old age. He is the listener of prayers. Please, Allah grant me, and my offspring serenity to pray at regular times and accept our prayers. Will you please, Allah, forgive me, my parents, and all the believers on the Day of the Resurrection?" Islam meaning is submission of faith to Allah, the creator of universe. After the death of the prophet Abraham the prophet Ishmael (Ismail) became prophet to the Arab nation of Makah and the surrounding towns of Hejaz.

The Prophet Lot (Lut)

The synopsis of the story of the prophet and messenger Lot (Lut) is according to the interpretation of Islamic resources. Allah saved the prophet Abraham (Ibrahim) and the prophet Lot (Lut) from the people of Babel. Allah guided them to the blessed holy land. Lot (Lut) was the nephew of the prophet and messenger Ibrahim. The prophets Lot (Lut) said, "I will go to the straight way of Allah. He is the wisest."

[The people of Lut (Lot) rejected the Messengers. Behold, their brother Lut said to them: "Will you not fear (Allah)? I am to you a Messenger worthy of all trust. So, fear Allah and obey me. No reward do I ask of you for it: my reward is only from the Lord of the worlds. Of all the creatures in the worlds, will you approach males, and leave those whom Allah has created for you to be your mate? Nay, you are a people transgressing (all limits)!" They said: "if you desist not, O Lut! you will assuredly be cast out!" He said: "I do detest your doings" (The Quran Translation, Ali, Yusuf 2007, 26: 160–175)].

The prophet Lot (Lut) submitted his faith to Allah, the creator of the universe. He lived in a village, the prophet Lot (Lut) advised the villagers for many years, saying, "I am an honest messenger of Allah to you. Believe me and follow me. Do you not fear Allah? You approach men (same-sex relationships), and you leave the women who were created by Allah for you. You all stand in the middle of the streets to practice mischief, and you practice sins of the same sex in your club."

The villagers rejected the message of Allah, the creator of the universe, and they said in arrogance, "Lot (Lut), if you do not stop your speeches, we will throw you out of our village."

"I would like to leave your village, but I am a prophet and messenger of Allah, the creator of the universe. The punishment of Allah will destroy the unbelievers and the sinners. I pray to Allah to save my family and me from the transgressors," the prophet Lot (Lut) said to the villagers.

"Bring us the punishment of your Allah if you are telling the truth. We will force you and your followers to get out of our village. You are using to purify," the villagers said in arrogance. The prophet Lot (Lut) said in his prayers, "Allah, the creator of the universe, help me against those villagers who practice sin, which never happened before, in the world, as you, Allah informed me. Allah, they rejected your message, and the men practice the sins of men approaching the same sex and leaving their women."

The angels' messengers of Allah went to the prophet Lot (Lut).

And he was exhausted by their visit because he felt weak from keeping them safe from the villagers. The angels said, "Lot (Lut), do not worry, and do not have sorrow. We are here to save you and your followers, except your wife. She will stay with those sinners because she deceived you. We will bring down punishment from the skies on the villagers because they have been extreme sinners and unbelievers. Then, we will place a visible sign for anyone who wants to understand." The villagers watched the angels; they thought that they were pretty men. They quickly came to the prophet Lot (Lut). Before that, they were in their club, practicing same-sex relationships. They said, "Lot (Lut), we told you to stop your speech and stop having visitors in your house."

"My people, these are my daughters; they are purifiers for you. Fear Allah, and do not put shame on me regarding my guests. Is there any man with you who has awareness?" the prophet messenger Lot (Lut) said to the villagers. "You know that we have nothing to do with your daughters, and you know what we want your guests of pretty men," the villagers said.

"If I have power, or if I can go to a strong supporter against you," the prophet and messenger Lot (Lut) said to the villagers. The angels said to Lot (Lut), "we are angels, messengers of Allah. Those people cannot reach you. Go with your family during the night, and do not look back. Your wife will stay with them. Their time will be in the morning. Is not the morning coming soon?"

[The people of Lut (Lot) rejected his warning. We sent against them a violent tornado with shower of stones, (which destroyed them), except Lut's household: We delivered them by early Dawn (The Quran Translation, Ali, Yusuf 2007, 54:33-39)].

According to the interpretation of Islamic resource, Allah saved the prophet Lot (Lut) and his family, except his wife. And Allah commanded the angels: to destruct the highest building of the village to be its lowest, and he rained down hot backed clay, as hard as rocks, from the skies. Allah's punishment was for the severe sinners.

The Prophet Joseph (Yusuf)

The synopsis of the story of the prophet Yusuf, or Joseph (peace on him) is according to the interpretation of Islamic resources. The prophet Joseph (Yusuf) was the son of the prophet Jacob (Yaqub) and the grandson of the prophet Isaac (Isehaq) and the great-grandson of the prophet Abraham (Ibrahim), (peace on them).

[Behold Joseph said to his father: "O my father! I saw eleven stars and the sun and the moon: I saw them prostrate themselves to me" (The Quran Translation, Ali, Yusuf 2007, 12: 4-110)].

"My father, in a dream I watched eleven planets, the sun, and the moon bow down to me," the prophet Joseph (Yusuf) said to his father, Jacob (Yaqub).

"Joseph do not tell your brothers. I'm afraid that they might arrange a cunning plan against you. Evil is an enemy to the humans. Allah will select you and teach you the speech of the holy book and wisdom. And Allah grants his grace to you and for the successors of Jacob (Yacub), such as he did for your great-grandfather Abraham (Ibrahim) and grandfather Isehaq (Isaac). Allah has the higher wisdom and knowledge," the prophet Jacob (Yaqub) said. Yusuf's half-brothers spoke to each other outdoors. "Joseph and his full brother are our father's favorites more than us, but we are a group of ten. Our father may have wondered mind. Let us kill Joseph (Yusuf) or leave him into an unknown area. Then, the care of our father will be given to us alone. There will be enough time for us to act moral."

"Do not slay Joseph. If you want to do something, put him in the desert at an empty water spring, and he will be taken by trippers," said one of Joseph's ten half-brothers.

"Why do you not permit us to take Joseph on a trip? We are his caregivers and advisers. Let him come with us tomorrow to play and have refreshments. We will take care of him," Joseph's ten half-brothers said to Jacob.

"I'm worried that if you take him on a trip, a wolf will kill him while you are not attending him," the prophet Jacob (Yaqub) said.

"If a wolf will kill him while we are a group of ten men, we are failures," Joseph's ten half-brothers said. The ten half-brothers accompanied Joseph on a trip, and they all decided to put Joseph (Yusuf) in the bottom of an empty water spring.

That night, the ten half-brothers arrived at their father, Jacob, crying and said, "our father, we went running and left Joseph with our stuff. A wolf killed and ate him. You may not believe us, but we say facts." And they gave Joseph's shirt, which they had marked with sheep's blood, to their father.

"This is a false story, I will have serenity, and I need the support of Allah, the creator of the universe," the prophet Jacob cried and spoke.

A group of trippers came, and they sent their waiter to bring water. He dropped his container into the empty water spring, and he said, "I have amazing news for you; here is a boy."

They hid Joseph, and they traded him for a little worth.

In Egypt, the man who had purchased Joseph said to his spouse, "manage his resident with kindness, he may assist us, or we can take him as a son."

According to the interpretation of Islamic resources, Allah sent the prophet Joseph (Yusuf) to Egypt and taught him the speech of the holy book and wisdom. Allah, the creator of the universe, has supremacy and authority over all matters, but most people do not know. When Joseph was in his full adulthood, Allah granted him strength and knowledge. Thus, he grants rewards to those who have morality. The wife of the master who bought Joseph wanted to make love with the prophet Joseph. She closed the doors and said, "come on, you are the beloved one." The master's wife desired him, but Joseph (Yusuf) realized the signs of Allah, the creator of the universe. Allah directed him to turn away from all evil's treks and from disgraceful behaviors. He was an honest servant and purified.

Joseph said, "Allah forbids adultery. He made my stay generous, and no grace came to those who made terrible sins."

They both ran towards the entrance of the room, and she cut up his clothes from the back. They both found her husband at the gate of the room. The master's wife said, "what is the penalty for one who has acted sinful touching of your wife. Send him to the jail for punishment." The prophet Joseph said, "she wanted to make love with me, but I rejected her."

One of her family was a witness and said, "if Joseph's clothing was cut in front, her story was true, and he was a liar, but if his clothing was cut on his back, she was a liar, and he was telling the truth."

He saw that Joseph's clothing was cut on the back; Joseph (Yusuf) had told the truth. Her husband said, "woman, it is your deception— the deception of women is massive. Joseph (Yusuf), forget about it. My wife, ask pardon of God for your sins. You have made mistakes." The ladies of the city talked with each other and said, "the wife of the master wanted to make love with her servant Joseph. She was excited with extreme love for him. We see that she is going off track." The master's wife knew of their gossip, and she invited them to have a meal in her house. She gave every one of them a sharp blade and fruit. The master's wife said to Joseph, "come here in front of the ladies." When the ladies of the city watched Joseph, they gasped, and they became fond of him. In their wonder, they cut wounds on their hands with the blades, and they said, "this is not a human; this is an angel." The master's wife said to them, "here is the one; you all blamed me. I wanted to make love with him, but he refused. And he keeps himself purified. And now, if he does not obey me, I will send him to the jail. What is better for him? Here or the company of the awful men in the jail?" The prophet Joseph (Yusuf) prayed to Allah: "the jail is better than that they are wanting me to do. Please turn me away from their trap. I do not want to share their sins."

According to the interpretation of Islamic resources, Allah listened to the prayer of the prophet Joseph (Yusuf), and he turned the women away from him. He listens and knows all things. The men of the city decided to send Joseph to the jail for years because of those women who made cut wounds on their hands. In the jail, there were two men as his companions. One of the two said, "in a vision of dream, I found myself making juice for wine."

The other man said, "In a dream, I found myself carrying food on my head, and the birds were eating it." "Clarify, the interpretation of these dreams. You are a man of reality," both of his friends in jail said.

"Before any diet is offered to you, I will tell you the type of food. It is part of my duty. I rejected the ways of people who do not believe in Allah, and they denied the Day of Resurrection. I use the belief of my father Jacob (Yaqub), my grandfather Isaac (Isehaq), and my great-grandfather Abraham (Ibrahim). We did not take any associates with Allah. Most people are not thankful. My two friends, I want to ask you: are the things you worship capable, or is Allah, the greatest? Allah is the higher power. You worship things, and you give them titles. You and your fathers are worshiping things that have no power. Allah has the higher power," the prophet Joseph (Yusuf) said.

According to the interpretation of Islamic resources, Joseph said to his friends, "Allah's order that you should worship Allah only. Most people do not realize the truth. My two friends in the jail, the explanations of your dreams are that one of you will dispense out the wine for his master to drink, and the other will be tied on a cross, and the birds will eat from his head. This is the interpretation of the dreams. The matter is done that you two requested."

"Ask forgiveness for me in your prayer," said the man who got freedom from the jail. Evil made Joseph (Yusuf), forgot to ask forgiveness of Allah for his friend. For that, Joseph remained in jail for additional years. The king of Egypt said to his chiefs, "I had a dream that seven large cows were eaten by seven slim cows, and there were seven green husks of whole grains of wheat and seven others dried husks. Explain the dream to me if you can understand it." "The dreams are unclear, and we are not familiar with explanation of the dreams," the chiefs said. "I know someone who can explain the dreams if you let me visit him. His name is Joseph (Yusuf)," said the man from the jail, now the waiter of the king of Egypt. The waiter went to Joseph and said, "you are a man of reality. Interpret the king of Egypt's dream, which is seven large cows that were eaten by seven slim cows, and seven green wheat grain husks and seven dried husks (wheat grains). The king wants to know the meaning." The prophet Joseph (Yusuf) said, "for seven years, the farmers will cultivate wheat grains. They should leave the crops of the wheat grains in the husks, except for a little quantity that they will use. During the seven years of droughts, they can eat what they stored, except the little that they guarded for planting. After the seven years of drought, a year will come in which the people will have plenty of water, and there will grow bountiful crops."

"Let Joseph come here," the king of Egypt said. The servant of the king visited Joseph and told him, "the king is waiting for you." The prophet Joseph (Yusuf) said, "go to your king, and ask him about the misconduct of the women who cut wounds in their hands? Allah, the creator of the universe, surely knows their misconduct."

"Women, what were your affair with Joseph?" the king of Egypt asked them.

They said there was no evil acting on him. The wife of the man who bought Joseph (Yusuf) said to the king of Egypt, "now, it is time for the true speech. I am the woman who wanted to make love with Joseph, and he refused. He was purified and moral. There was no evil acting on him. God knows that I did not deceive my husband before that time. God will not guide the bad manner of sinners. I do not pardon myself. The human soul sometime acts such as evil, except if Allah grants mercy to, he or she." "Bring Joseph here. I will take him to serve me," the king of Egypt said to his chiefs. Joseph went to the king, who said, "feel safe today. You are in my kingdom. I am the highest authority of Egypt." "Please King, put me over the treasures of the kingdom of Egypt. I will be guard to it, as one who knows its value," the prophet Joseph said. According to the Islamic resources, Allah granted the prophet Joseph (Yusuf) the chance to have this honored position. Allah grants rewards to those who attain morality. The rewards of the eternal garden are the best for those who believe. They will have an endless, joyful lifestyle. One day, Joseph's ten half-brothers entered his presence. He knew them, but they did not know him. Joseph ordered his workers to give his brothers a good harvest. And he said, "if you bring me your brother from your father and a stepmother, I will reward you full camel load of grains and more. If you do not bring him, you will not have a cup of grains from me. I will not permit you to come here again."

"We will ask the permission of our father," Joseph's ten half-brothers said. The prophet Joseph said to his workers, "put their products into their bags." The ten half-brothers said to their father, Jacob, "Our father, we will not have a future harvest of grains except if we accompany our brother from our stepmother. We want him to go with us. They will give us full measures of harvests, and we will take care of him."

"I cannot depend on you with him because I depended on you with Joseph (Yusuf), and we lost him. Allah is the keeper, and he is gracious," Jacob said. They opened their bags; they found their products were returned to them.

"Our father, what is more than that? Our products of trade are returned to us. We will get extra food for our family, and we will keep the safety of our brother. And they will add a full amount of camel's weight to our harvests," Joseph's ten half-brothers said.

"I will not let him go with you unless you say an oath in the name of Allah that you will bring him back to me—except if you are surrounded by danger and become helpless," Jacob said.

They said an oath in the name of Allah. And Allah was the witness.

"My sons do not enter in same gate; you shall enter by several gates. I cannot protect you with my advice. Allah is the only one who orders in the heaven. I put my hope in Allah, and let us all put our hope in him," Jacob said. According to the Islamic resources, if they entered from several gates, that would not protect them from Allah's plan, but it was Jacob's inquiry in his heart. Allah placed his commands. He has all knowledge and full capability, but most people do not realize. They arrived, and the prophet Joseph said to his full brother, "set here. I am your full brother: Do not be afraid of what others are making."

After Joseph's workers gave them the measures of harvests, Joseph (Yusuf) placed the gold cup of the king of Egypt into his full brother's bags. A man said, "people of camels, you all are thieves."

"What are you looking for?" Joseph's ten half-brothers said.

"We are looking for a gold cup of the king of Egypt; we used it in measuring crops. A reward of a camel load for who finds it," one of Joseph's workers said. "You know well that we did not come to make disruption in the land, and we did not take it," Joseph's ten half-brothers said.

"What will be the consequence if we find out that you are liars?" Joseph's worker asked.

"We arrest the criminal to compensate for the law-breaking. That is how we punish the wrong one," Joseph's ten half-brothers said.

According to the Islamic resources, Joseph searched in the bags of his ten half-brothers. After that, he brought the king's gold cup out of his full brother's bag. Allah planned to Joseph (Yusuf) saving his full brother. Allah advances the level of wisdom to whom he will. Allah's knowledge is above all.

"If he is thief, he had a full brother been a thief before," Yusuf's ten half-brothers said.

Joseph kept the secret in his mind and did not reveal to them that he was their half-brother. "You have the wickedest attitude, and Allah knows well the truth of what you proclaim," the prophet Joseph said to them.

"Master, his father is an aged, ill man, and he will get sad for missing him. Keep one of us. We see that you are generous," the ten half-brothers said. "Allah prohibits arresting of someone other than the thief with whom we found our stuff. If I detain another one, I will act unjustly," Joseph said. They knew that there was no hope. They talked of a distant place. We know that our father took a sincere oath in the name of Allah because we did not keep Joseph." The older half-brother of Joseph said, "in the name of Allah, I will not go out from this land of Egypt until my father agrees, and after Allah's order. Go back to your father. Tell him that his son stole the gold measuring cup of the king of Egypt. We could not be protectors against the hidden. And let him ask the people of the city where we went, and the group who was with us. He will find out that we said facts." Joseph's nine half-brothers went to their father and told him that his son stole the gold measuring cup of the king.

Jacob cried and said, "your story fits you, and I will have serenity and patience. May be Allah will send them back to me. Allah has all the wisdom and knowledge. How great is my sadness from missing Joseph." Jacob's eyes turned white with agony, and he felt unhappy.

"You will never miss the remembrance of Joseph until you have critical illness or until you die," Jacob's sons said to their father.

"I tell my weakness and sadness to Allah, and I know from Allah what you do not know. My children, ask about Joseph and his brother, and never give up. Have hope in Allah. No one should loss hope on Allah's mercy, except the unbelievers," Jacob said.

The ten half-brothers came back and said to Joseph, "honor, sorrow has involved our family and us. Now, we have brought some cash to pay for the king's golden cup. We prayed and asked for help."

"Do you know in what manner you made Joseph (Yusuf), and his full brother suffer when you committed bad conduct?" the prophet Joseph said to his ten half-brothers.

"Is this Joseph (Yusuf)?" his ten half-brothers asked in astonishment.

"Yes, Joseph (Yusuf), and this is my full brother. Allah has been gracious to us. Whoever has good morals and has patience will never get agonized and will win the recompenses of the eternal garden," the prophet Joseph said.

"Allah has favored you more than us, and we are guilty," Joseph's ten half-brothers said.

"Today we ask forgiveness and mercy of Allah. I wish that Allah will forgive your sins. I will ask him to pardon you all. He is gracious and a forgiver to those who repent. Take my shirt and throw it on my father's face. His vision will be healed. Then, you all come back here with your families," the prophet Joseph said.

The prophet Jacob (Yaqub) asked when his sons returned home, "I feel the odor of Joseph. What do you think? Am I mindless?"

"You have an old mind," his sons said.

According to the Islamic resources, the good news came to the prophet Jacob (Yacub). One of his sons threw Joseph's shirt over Jacob's face, and the miracle of Allah healed Jacob's vision. "I told you that I know from Allah, the creator of the universe, things you do not recognize," Jacob said. "Our father prays to Allah to forgive us. In the matter of Joseph, we were severe sinners," Jacob's sons said.

"I will pray to Allah to forgive you all. He is most merciful and compassionate," Jacob said. When they arrived in Egypt, Joseph provided a residence home for his parents with him. "You all are welcome in Egypt. Feel secure if Allah permits," the prophet Joseph said to his parents and his brothers. According to the Islamic resources, the prophet Joseph raised the hands of his father and his mother high on his throne. They all prostrated themselves to Allah in gratefulness.

"My father, Jacob, this is the explanation of the vision in my dream. Allah made it true. He loves me. He gave me freedom from jail, and you all came here from the desert, even after evil spread hostility while my ten half-brothers were hating me. Allah knows all the things hidden that he plans to do. Allah has all knowledge and wisdom: He gave me strength and taught me the interpretation of dreams and events. Allah is the creator of the heavens, earth, and every natural thing in between. Allah, please, protect me during my life and after life. Take my soul at death as a the one who submitted his faith to Allah and place me with the virtuous people," the prophet Joseph (Yusuf) said.

[Such is one of the stories of what happened unseen, which We reveal it by inspiration unto you: nor were you (present) with them when they concerted their plan together in the process of weaving their plots (The Quran Translation, Ali, Yusuf 2007, 12: 102-111)].

The messenger prophet Muhamad was not present with Joseph's ten half-brothers when they decided together to slay Joseph (Yusuf).

The prophet Muhamad received the original story of Joseph (Yusef), in the Arabic Holy Quran. Many people do not have faith in Allah, the creator of universe. The message of the prophet Muhamad is to humans and jinn (unseen). The prophets did not ask people for a recompence for this. How many signs do the people see in the heavens and on earth, but they turn their heads? Many people around the world believe in, the creator of the universe, but they associate other things or partners with him, while the prophet Muhamad and the believers worship Allah only.

The Prophet Shuaib

The following is a synopsis of the story of the prophet Shuaib (peace on him), according to the interpretation of Islamic resources, Allah sent the prophet Shuaib to the people of Madyan.

[To the Madyan people (We sent) Shuaib, one of their brothers: he said: "O my people worship Allah: you have no other god but Him. And do not give short measure in weight: I see you in prosperity, but I fear for you the Penalty in a Day that will compass (you) all round" (The Quran Translation, Ali, Yusuf 2007, 11:84-95)].

Shuaib said, "my people of Madyan, you should worship Allah, the creator of the heavens, earth, and everything in-between. You should expect the Day of Resurrection. Do not commit abuse or spread exploitation on the earth. You have no other divine but Allah. You should have faith in him. Visible signs have come to you from him. Give a fair and balanced measure and weight. Do not withhold from people their belongings, and do not disrupt the earth after it settles on rules. Do not threaten people on the roads, delaying them from the path of the right faith. You were small numbers, and Allah increased your numbers. Remember the end of those who committed sins. If you are divided into two groups—believers and unbelievers—wait until Allah judges both of you. He is the best judge."

"We will force you to get out of our city and those who believe you. You all must return to our beliefs," the arrogant leaders said to the prophet Shuaib.

"We should not formulate a lie against Allah, we will not return to your mistaken religion. Allah has rescued us from your confusions. Allah, the creator of the universe, can reach everything by his knowledge, and we trust him only," Shuaib and the believers said to the unbelievers of Madyan.

"If we follow Shuaib, we will be destroyed," the leaders of the rejecters said.

"My people, I conveyed the messages to you. I offered you a direction to Allah's straight path. And I will not grieve over a people who are unbelievers," Shuaib said. "Does your religion command us to leave the statues of our gods, which we worship as our fathers worshipped? And you want us to leave—what should we do with our stuff? You must withhold burdens. You have religious madness," the rejecters of Madyan said.

"My people, I have a visible sign from Allah. He has given me wisdom and good morals. I do not want to be against you. I want the best for you, and your success is my duty. I trust Allah only. My people do not let your denial to me cause you to commit sins. I am worried that you will have punishment similar to the nations of the prophets Noah (Nuh), Hud (Houd), Salish (Saleh), and Lot (Lut). They were near you. Ask forgiveness and turn to Allah in repentance. Allah is the most gracious and generous," the messenger Shuaib said. "We do not comprehend what you are saying. You have no strength among us unless your family, we must stone you to death. You have no worth among us," the rejecters said.

"My people, are my family and I more vital to you than Allah? You forgot Allah with condemnation. He knows all that you do. My people, do whatever you want. I will do my part. You will know soon who is just, who falls in the penalty of degradation, and who is a liar. If you wait, I am also waiting with you," Shuaib said.

According to the interpretation of Islamic resources, most the people of nation of the prophet Shuaib rejected the message of Allah.

And in the morning, Allah sent a grievous earthquake that grasped all the rejecters. They lay prostrate in their houses. The punishment to those who took protectors other than Allah was critical. They acted like the spider who builds for itself a house, but the spider's house is very fragile. Allah knows everything. He is exalted in power and wise. Allah saved the prophet Shuaib and those who believed with him by mercy. Then a massive punishment grabbed the unbelievers. Their homes became as if they had never lived there. The rejecters in Madyan were destroyed, such as the rejecters of Thamud people were destroyed.

All the people who rejected the prophet Shuaib's message were vanished. Allah saved those who understood and who had the knowledge. In this story, there are signs to the people who understand.

The Wise Luqman

The synopsis of the story of the Wise Luqman (peace on him). According to the interpretation of Islamic resources. Allah granted Wisdom to Luqman. He praised Allah, the creator of the universe, and He was man of truth. He showed gratitude and knew that whoever showed gratefulness to Allah would earn rewards and mercy to his or her soul.

[Behold, Luqman said to his son by way of Instruction: "O my son! Do not join in worship (others) with Allah: for false worship that is indeed the highest wrongdoing" (The Quran Translation, Ali, Yusuf 2007, 31:13-23]).

According to the interpretation of Islamic resources, the commands of Allah to human are: to honor his or her parents. If the parents wanted him or her to associate with Allah in worship, he or she should not obey them, but he or she should still care for them.

The Wise Luqman advised his son and said, "my son, you should not associate with Allah, the creator of the universe, in worshiping. My son, if a very small seed of mastery is hidden in a rock, in the heavens or in the earth, Allah can bring it. My son: keep regular prayers justice and have patience in whatever happens to you. You should not move your check up to the people—do not act superior. Walk in quietness on the earth without arrogance. Allah does not love arrogant and does not love overjoyed individuals. Ease your voice—the worst sound is the sound of the donkey."

The Messenger Moses (Musa)

The synopsis of the story of the messenger Moses (Musa), (peace on him), is according to the interpretation of Islamic resources. In ancient Egypt's land, the pharaoh positioned himself arrogant, and he made the Egyptian people separate into parties. The pharaoh oppressed groups of them. His soldiers tortured the children of Israel with the worst torment, slaughtered their male infants, and kept their females alive. The reason was that the pharaoh's chiefs told him that a man from the seeds of Israel would kill him. A mother from the children of Israel was afraid that the pharaoh would kill her infant Moses (Musa). According to the interpretation of Islamic resources, she got an order from Allah to feed Moses her breast milk, put him in a wooden box, and then put the box in the Nile River. And she should not fear or grieve. She got a promise that Allah would bring Moses (Musa) back and make him one of the prophets and messengers. And she fulfilled the order of Allah. Allah directed the waves of the Nile River to move Moses to the other coast.

[And has the story of Moses reached you? (The Quran Translation, Ali, Yusuf 2007, 20: 9-112)].

Pharaoh's wife was sitting on the other side of the Nile river. She watched a wooden box floating on the water. She ordered her guards to bring her the box. Moses (Musa) was taken up by an enemy against Allah. Moses (Musa) was from the offspring of the prophets Abraham (Ibrahim), Isaac (Isehaq), and Jacob (Yacub). The guards of the pharaoh's wife opened the box, and they were astonished when they found a male infant.

"Moses (Musa) is a relief for my eyes, do not slay him. He may help us, or we can keep him as a son," the pharaoh's wife said to her husband.

Allah granted love to Moses (Musa) and wisdom. He would become an enemy to the pharaoh and his followers, and he would become a cause of their sorrow. Pharaoh, his chief Haman, and their soldiers were serious sinners. The heart of Moses's mother became empty. She thought to tell the matter concerning Moses (Musa). She was one of the faithful believers. "Look for Moses," said Moses's mother, as she sent his sister to check on her son. His sister observed Moses from a distance, and the security guards did not see her. Allah caused Moses to refuse all the wet-nurses (women who have breast milk).

"Would you like me to show you a woman who could be a wet-nurse to the infant?" Moses's sister asked the pharaoh's security guards, and they agreed.

According to the Islamic resources, Allah assured the heart of the mother of Moses (Musa); Allah's miracle happened: Moses (Musa) came back to his mother, so her eyes might be pleased, and she stopped feeling sad. She knew that the promise of Allah, the creator of the universe, was real, but most people did not know. The prophet and messenger Moses matured up strong man and clever; Allah bestowed to him knowledge. He gave rewards to the people of good morals.

The prophet and messenger Moses (Musa) arrived at a time when everyone was busy. Two men were fighting—one from the children of Israel and one from his enemy, pharaoh's people. The one from his belief asked for help against the one from his enemy. Moses hit the enemy accidentally, and he unintentionally killed him.

"This was an act of Satan (evil), who misled me. I have harmed myself. Allah, the creator of the universe, forgive me. I will never be an assistant to the criminals," Moses said.

Allah forgave Moses (Musa) and released him from sadness. He is the forgiver and gracious. The prophet Moses was waiting and was afraid of the consequences. The one who wanted his help on the previous day cried again.

"You are a troublemaker," Moses said. And Moses wanted to hit the other man from his enemy.

"Do you intend to kill me as you murdered a man yesterday? You want to be an oppressor on the earth, and you want to be unfair," the other man from his enemy said. After a while, a man came hurrying from the far end of the city. He said, "Moses (Musa), the pharaoh's chiefs are conferring about you, and they intend to kill you. Run off the town. I am honest to you."

Moses left the city hurrying; he was afraid and said in his prayer, "Allah, please save me from the oppression of the pharaoh and his soldiers, amen."

Moses went toward the east to Madyan city and prayed. "Allah, please guide me to the straight way. And thank you, Allah, for saving me."

Moses came to a well of water in Madyan, he watched a crowd of people waiting in order to fill their water containers. And on the side, there were two girls, they were waiting to fill their containers.

"What is the matter with you?" Moses (Musa) asked the two girls.

"We cannot get water until the men finish filling their water containers, and our father is an old man," one of the two girls said. The prophet Moses (Musa) filled their water containers. Afterward, he went to sit in the shade. Moses said in his prayer, "Allah, I will go to anywhere you want me to go."

One of the two girls walked quietly to Moses and said, "my father is inviting you; he wants to give you recompense for filling our water containers."

Moses went to her old father and told him the story of his killing one of his enemies.

"Do not be afraid here," the father of the two girls said. "Allah saved you from the sinners."

"My father, hire him. He is a strong and honest man," the quiet girl said.

"I will be glad if you marry one of my daughters. On that cause, you shall assist me for eight years, but if you fulfill ten, it will be a favor from you. I do not like to place you in a complicated situation. If Allah wills, you will find me among the trustworthy people," the father said.

"This is an honest agreement between me and you. I will complete either of the two terms. There is no injustice to me, and Allah is the witness over what we say," the prophet Moses (Musa) said.

The prophet Moses chose to marry the quiet girl. After Moses had completed his years of serving her father, he was sitting with his family and saw a fire tree from the direction of the mountain. Moses said, "stay here. I see a fire tree. I can bring burning wood from the fire to you for warmth."

[But when he came to the fire, a voice was heard O Moses! Verily I am your Lord! Therefore (in My presence) put off your shoes you are in the sacred valley Tuwa. I have chosen you: Listen, then, to the inspiration (sent to you). Verily, I am Allah. There is no God but I: so, serve me only and establish regular prayer celebrating My praise. Verily the Hour is coming – My design is to keep it hidden- for every soul to receive its reward by the measure of its endeavor (The Quran Translation, Ali, Yusuf 2007, 20:11-103)].

According to the interpretations of Islamic resources, Allah, the creator of the universe, talked directly to the prophet Moses (Musa); when he came near the fire tree (bush). Allah called Moses (Musa) from the right side of the holy valley Tuwa, on a blessed spot. Allah told Moses (Musa) to take his shoes off. Allah chose him and instructed him that there is no God but Allah, (the creator of the heavens, earth, and everything in between). And There is no divine except Allah. Moses should worship Allah only, pray regularly for remembrance, and praise Allah. And Moses should know that the hour of the Day of Resurrection is coming. Allah keeps the time of the last hour of the Day of Resurrection undisclosed. Every soul will receive the consequences by the measure of his or her acts. And Moses should not follow the unbelievers; they follow evil; they are away from morality, and they will die. Allah questioned Moses (Musa), what was in his right hand?

"This is my rod. I use it as a crutch, and I use it to beat down leaves of trees for my lambs, and it has other uses," Moses fearfully said to Allah. According to the interpretation of Islamic resources, Allah told Moses (Musa) to throw his rod down. Then, Moses threw his rod down, and it was turned into a huge snake that moved actively. And Allah told Moses to grasp it, and do not be afraid. Allah turned the snake back to a rod. And Allah told Moses (Musa) to put his hand to the side under his arm. It will turn white without illness. Put it there again, and it will return as before. Moses put his hand under his arm; it turned white. He put it back; it returned as it had been. This was another sign.

According to the interpretation of Islamic resources, Allah told Moses (Musa) to go to the pharaoh of Egypt because he oppressed people and to show him these two of Allah's signs.

"Please, Allah, strength my chest, ease my mission, and remove the twitch that impairs my tongue. So, they can comprehend my talking. And appoint an associate from my family, my brother Aaron (Haroun). He has more fluent speech. Increase my power through him and make him share my responsibility. I fear that they will deny me. I need my brother Aaron as supporter to validate me. We will glorify you and praise you regularly, as you watch over people forever," Moses said to Allah.

Allah granted Moses (Musa) his request. Allah preferred Moses (Musa) when his sister said to the guards of the pharaoh, "would you like me to inform you of wet nurse who can have breast milk for him?" Allah sent back Moses to his mother that she might be satisfied, and she did not feel sad. When Moses reached his full strength as a man, he accidentally killed a man. Allah saved him from the revenge of his enemies and tested him in different situations. Moses (Musa) remained for years among the people of Madyan.

The prophet and messenger Moses (Musa) went to the holy valley Tuwa. Allah talked to Moses directly and made Moses serve Him. In the interpretation of Islamic resources, Allah told Moses and his brother Aaron (Haroun): "to go, both of them, with the two signs of Allah to the pharaoh, and praise Allah. The pharaoh transgressed; they should speak with him softly. The pharaoh should know, and he should fear Allah."

"I afraid that the pharaoh will penalize us or harm us, I killed a man from the pharaoh's people, and I fear that they may kill me," Moses said to Allah.

According to the interpretation of Islamic resources, Allah told Moses (Musa) not to be afraid. Allah was with both of them watching. And Allah ordered them to go to the pharaoh and tell him, "we are the messengers of Allah, the creator of the universe. Release the children of Israel, and do not torture them. We have come to you with signs and peace on whoever follows Allah's direction." Both messengers Moses and Aaron received the sacred Torah, and whoever denied their message would have the punishment of Allah.

Moses and his brother Aaron went to the pharaoh with the two signs of Allah and said, "we are the messengers of Allah, the creator of the universe. Release the children of Israel, and do not torture them. We are here to show you two clear signs. And peace is on whoever follows the straight way. Allah sent both of us to tell you that the penalty awaits those who reject the faith of Allah."

"Who is Allah?" Pharaoh asked.

"Allah is the creator of the universe, gives everything its justice. He created the heavens, the earth, and everything natural in between and guides us. You should believe," Moses said.

"What about the previous generations and centuries?" Pharaoh asked. "The knowledge of the previous generations is with Allah in holy book, in the heavens. Allah never makes error, and he never forgets. Allah made the earth like a flooring spread out. He has enabled you to go by roads and channels. He has sent down water from the sky. He has produced various pairs of plants, each sign for whoever has a mind to understand. On the earth, Allah created you from dust. You will die, and your soul will return to Allah. He will resurrect you again to life on the Day of Resurrection," Moses said.

"I am your highest god, if you worship anyone other than me, I will send you and your brother to jail," the pharaoh said.

"Even if I bring manifest signs of proof to you?" the prophet and messenger Moses (Musa) asked.

"Bring it, if you are saying the truth," the pharaoh said.

Moses (Musa) showed pharaoh and his chiefs the signs of Allah, the creator of the universe. Moses (Musa) threw down his rod, and it turned to a giant snake. He grasped it; it turned into a rod again. He put his hand under his arm, and it turned white without disease. He put it under his arm again; it returned as it had appeared before. The pharaoh and his close chiefs laughed, and said, "Moses is a skilled witch."

The pharaoh said, "He would like to move you out of your lands by his magical tricks. What is your advice?"

"Wait to check him and his brother and send to the cities to collect every skilled witch," the chiefs of the pharaoh replied.

"Did not we adopt you amongst us as an infant? And you lived with us for years. And you committed a crime of killing a man. Now, you are not grateful," the pharaoh said to Moses.

"I did a crime while I was with those who went off track. And I escaped from you when I feared you. Allah, the creator of the universe granted me wisdom, messages, and appointed me as one of the prophets and messengers. And you have enslaved the children of Israel," Moses said.

"The messenger who was sent to you is crazy. Do you hear him? Do we believe two men whose families are from our slaves?" the pharaoh said in haughty to his people.

"Allah created the east and the west and everything in between. Allah is your creator and the creator of your forefathers," the prophet Moses said.

"Moses, do you come to get us out of our lands with your magical tricks? We can do magical work to match your magical tricks. Make a date between you and us, which we will not fail to keep. In a certain place, you and we will have equal chances," the pharaoh said.

"The appointed time is on the day of the ceremony. Let the people to gather when the sun is shining." Moses said. The chiefs of the pharaoh collected the skilled magicians for the appointed day, and a lot of people gathered. The pharaoh and his people put together their designs. The prophet and messenger Moses and Aaron came back on the day of ceremony. "Are there gifts for us if we are the winner?" the magicians asked the pharaoh. The pharaoh said, "you all will be my favorites."

"Do not fabricate lies against Allah. He will destroy you with torment," the prophet Moses (Musa) said to the magicians.

The witches whispered with each other over their magic work, but they kept their talk secret, "These two men are experts, in magical tricks. Their goal is to move you out from your land with their witchcraft and to destroy your unique techniques. Show your plan of magical tricks and gather in line. Today, the winner will have the superior hand."

The magicians then asked Moses, "will you throw first or we?"

"You all throw first," Moses (Musa) said. The magicians threw their ropes. Moses watched their magical tricks—rods and ropes moving as live snakes.

According to the Islamic resources, Moses felt fear. Allah inspired to Moses (Musa), "do not be afraid; you have the upper hand. Throw what you grasp in your right hand." Moses (Musa) threw his rod; it turned to a huge snake that swallowed all the fabricated magical tricks. The works of the magicians would never be fruitful. All the magicians prostrated themselves to Allah and said, "we believe in Allah. He is our creator. He is the creator of the heavens, earth, and everything in between."

Pharaoh got angry and said, "you believe in his God before I allow to you? Moses is your boss, who has trained you. I will cut your hands and feet, and I will crucify you all on palm trees. You all will know who can give severe and long-lasting punishments."

The magicians said to pharaoh, "we will not favor you more than Allah, who created us. His signs came to us. Decide whatever you desire to verdict. You can only judge in the life of this world. We believe in Allah. He may pardon our sins and forgive us for the magical tricks that you forced us to do. Allah is the greatest and eternal absolute one. On the Day of Resurrection, anyone who comes to him as an extreme sinner will go to the fire of hell. In the fire, he will neither die nor live. Whoever comes as a believer and has worked in good manner, Allah will purify him or her from evil, and he or she will have rewards. The winners will live in the garden of Eden, which includes flowing rivers. We hope that Allah forgives our sins because we joined the first believers." "No matter whatever signs which you bring to us from your magical tricks; we will not believe you," the pharaoh and his people said to the messenger Moses. The pharaoh wanted to kill his wife because she believed in Allah. She prayed, "Allah, please, save me from the pharaoh and his evil works. Please save me from his oppression and grant me a house in the eternal garden."

Allah sent two messengers to the pharaoh—the messenger Moses (Musa), and his brother Aaron (Haroun). Pharaoh disobeyed the messengers. Allah gave the pharaoh damaging punishments. Allah punished the pharaoh's people with years of deprivation and deficiency of crops, that they should remember the justice. If a bad condition affected them, they thought that a magical trick was done by Moses (Musa) and his followers. If something good happened to them, they said, "this is our good work." All the wealth is with Allah, but most people do not know. Pharaoh and his people were arrogant and criminals. Allah, the creator of the universe, sent to pharaoh and his people nine signs. Two signs were with Moses (Musa), the rod that turned into a snake, and Moses's hand turning white without harm and the other seven signs were punishments—years of droughts or shortening of crops, epidemic disease and animals with plague, flooding of the Nile River, and the spread of lice, locusts, frogs, and bloody Nile water. Allah's punishments were to the pharaoh and his people, the pharaoh said to Moses, "pray to your Allah, by what he has promised you, to remove the plague and the punishment from us. We will believe you, and we will send the children of Israel with you."

The pharaoh was the leader of the dangers. Then, Allah sent the messenger Moses (Musa) with visible signs to the pharaoh, Haman, and Korah (Karon). When Moses (Musa) brought them the truth, they said, "Moses is a witch and a liar." The pharaoh and his followers killed the sons of those who believed and kept their women alive. Allah sent punishments to those who caused exploitation on the earth. Allah showed them signs and detained them with conditions that they might return to faith.

After that, Allah removed the punishment from them. The pharaoh and his followers continued their arrogance without right. They broke the promised word. They saw every sign, but they did not believe it. They saw the way of wisdom, but they did not accept it. When they saw the way of silliness; they accepted it. They had rejected and neglected Allah's signs. For those who rejected Allah's signs and who refused to believe in the Day of the Resurrection, their arrangements were worthless. They would be judged for what they used to do.

"Allah knows more than me or you. He knows who has upright direction. And the sinners fail," the prophet Moses said to the pharaoh and his people. Pharaoh said to his nation, "I do not tell you except that I see the righteous. And I direct you to the truthful path. Let me kill Moses, I fear that he will change your religion, or he will cause exploitation on the lands."

According to Islamic resources, one of the believers from the family of pharaoh who hid his faith, said, "do you want to kill Moses just because he said that his divine is Allah, the creator of the universe? Moses (Musa) has brought visible signs to you. If he is lying, upon him is the consequence of his lie, but if he is truthful, Allah will strike you with punishments. Allah does not guide the transgressors or the liars. My people, today the authority is yours as high leaders on earth. But who would protect you from the punishment of Allah? I fear that you will have torment such as Noah's people, Aad's people, and Thamud's people and those after them. Allah offer justice for his servants. My people, I'm afraid that you will be punished on the Day of Resurrection. There will not be any protector from the punishment. Allah does not let a person go astray without an invitation to righteousness. And the prophet Joseph came to you with visible signs, but you disbelieved in which he brought until he died. You all said, Allah, the creator of the universe, would never send a messenger prophet again. My people, obey me. I will direct you to the way of Allah, the creator of the universe. My people, this world of life is only temporary gratification. Thus, the eternal garden is the home of permanent settlement. If one acts evil, he or she will not be rewarded. So, whoever behaves virtuously, whether male or female, will enter the gardens of Eden. There will be a given establishment without an account. My people, I invite you to the savior way while you invite me to go hellfire. You wanted to stop believing in Allah, the creator of the universe, and associate with him. And I invite you to believe in Allah. He is the forgiver. Your invitation to me has no response; our return is to him. I trust my matters with Allah. The transgressors will be companions in the hellfire. You will remember what I am saying to you. Allah is watching his servants, and he protects the believers from the evil one's plans. Those who rejected the signs without knowledge or authority are sinners in the sight of Allah, and they are haters in the sight of those who have believed. Allah put seals over every heart that belongs to an arrogant dictator unbeliever."

The pharaoh deceived his people, and they obeyed him. They were disobedient to Allah, the creator of the universe. The pharaoh said, "Moses invented magic tricks only, and we have not heard of this belief among our forefathers. My people, does not the treasures of Egypt are mine? And these rivers are streaming in my lands. Do you not see? Am I not grateful more than this man, who is irrelevant and has difficulty expressing himself in speech? Why has his Allah not placed upon him jewelries of gold from the heavens? Why did he not come with angels in groups? My chiefs, you have no other divine, but me. My chief Haman, burn for me; make a fire upon clay of dust and construct for me a tower that I might reach the way to the heavens. I want to see Allah, the God of Moses (Musa), but Moses is a liar." Satan (evil) made the tricks of the pharaoh attractive, and the pharaoh avoided the straight path. Pharaoh did not expect destruction of his design. Pharaoh sent among the cities to recruit soldiers, and he said, "Moses and his followers are few gangs, and they are frustrating us. We are safeguarding society; we must kill them."

"I ask protection of Allah from every arrogant person who does not believe in the Day of Resurrection," the prophet Moses prayed.

[Then We told Moses by Inspiration: "Strike the sea with your rod." So, it divided, and each separate part became like the huge, firm mass of mountain. And We made the other

party approach there. We delivered Moses and all who were with him; but We drowned the others. Verily in this a Sign: but most of them do not believe (The Quran Translation, Ali, Yusuf 2007, 26:63-68)].

The design of the pharaoh and unbelievers was not fulfilled.

The commands of Allah to the messenger Moses (Musa) were: to hit the Red Sea with the rod, and a dry pathway will appear in the red sea. To go with the believers, do not feel frightened of being struck by the pharaoh and do not be terrified of sinking in water.

At sunrise, when they all saw one another, the children of Israel said, "we will be vanished by pharaoh and his soldiers."

"Allah is with us. He will help me," the prophet and messenger Moses (Musa) said.

In the name of Allah, the prophet Moses (Musa) hit the sea with his rod. The sea parted in two, and each portion was like a great high mountain. Allah settled a dry pathway and saved Moses (Musa) and his followers. The pharaoh and his soldiers followed them. The pharaoh directed his people to the hell and led his people off track. He did lead them to the safe way.

Allah made the pharaoh's soldiers sink in the Red Sea and kept the body of the dead pharaoh; that was a great sign. The Red Sea's waters covered pharaoh's soldiers. Allah removed the pharaoh and his soldiers from gardens that had rivers, treasures, and honorable positions. Allah rewarded the believers to inherit that. Thus, Allah caused the people who had been oppressed to inherit the east and west regions of the lands, which were blessed. Allah made the body of the pharaoh to be pushed to the beach of the Red Sea. The ancient Egyptians made him a mummy, as a reminder sign of who did not believe.

Korah (Karon)

Korah (Karon, Qaroun) was from the children of Israel, but he oppressed them. Allah gave wealth to Korah (Karon). The keys of his treasures were heavy loads for strong men.

Infront his people, Korah came wearing jewelries and surrounded by wealth. A group of children of Israel said, "we wish to have such as was given to Korah (Karon)."

The rabbis of the children of Israel said, "grief to you all. The rewards of the eternal garden are better for those who believe and have morality. And none is given the reward of the eternal garden except the people who have patience in life."

"You should thank Allah for what he gave you. Not overjoying in your life. Allah does not love overjoyed people. The eternal gardens of the delights are better. And do not forget your portion in life. Ensure generosity because Allah gave you wealth and treasures. Do not make wrongdoings on the earth. Allah does not like the transgressors," the good community of Korah (Karon) advised him.

"I was given my wealth and treasure because I have the expertise," Korah (Karon) said with arrogance.

Did Korah (Karon) not realize that Allah demolished people, before him who were stronger in power and richer in treasures? Or did Korah think that the criminals would not be asked for their crimes?

Allah, the creator of the universe, made Korah (Karon), his treasures, wealth, and his palace sink down in the earth by an earthquake. No one could help him; they did not protect themselves. Allah expands wealth to whoever of his servants as he wills.

The people who had desired Korah (Karon) position during his wealth now said, "Allah preferred us over him. He did not order the earth to absorb us, such as Korah (Karon). The unbelievers did not win. Allah will give the rooms of the paradise to those who do not want superiority on the earth or transgressors."

The Plague

The people of pharaoh were surrounded by damaging punishments. Allah destroyed Korah (Karon), pharaoh, and Haman because they were arrogant in the lands. Allah sent Moses (Musa) to them with visible signs; they refused to believe, but they could not escape Allah's punishment. Allah punished them for their sins. Among them, were those who were punished by a storm of stones; those who were apprehended by plague; those who the earth swallowed them such as Korah (Karon), and those who sank in water such as pharaoh. Allah did not aggravate them, but they aggravated themselves. Pharaoh and his soldiers were wrongdoers in the lands without right, and they thought they would not return to Allah. They rejected Allah's signs and were neglectful. Allah threw pharaoh and his soldiers into the Red Sea. See how the end was for the severely sinners? And on the Day of Resurrection, they would not be helped. A curse took them.

The children of Israel unknowing

The children of Israel who crossed the Red Sea with prophet Moses (Musa) came near a group of people who were worshipping statues. The children of Israel asked the prophet Moses (Musa) to make a statue for them to worship, just like those people.

[We took the Children of Israel (with safety) across the sea. They came upon a people devoted entirely to some idols they had. They said: "O Moses fashion for us a god like unto the gods they have." He said: "surely you are a people without knowledge" (The Quran Translation, Ali, Yusuf 2007, 7:138-141)].

"You are unknowing people. Do you want me to make a god other than Allah, the creator of the universe, for you to worship? Allah has preferred you all over the worlds," Moses said. Those worshippers of the statue were destroyed because they were involved in the worst of what they were doing.

The appointment

According to the interpretation of Islamic resources, Allah commanded Moses (Musa) to go to Sinai on Altor Mountain for forty nights. "Take my place among the children of Israel, ensure good morals, and do not follow the way of the sinners," the prophet Moses said to his brother Aaron (Haroun). When Moses arrived at the appointed time, he said, "praise is to you, Allah, the creator of the universe. Will you please show me yourself; I want to see you?"

According to the interpretation of Islamic resources, Allah told to Moses (Musa) that his eyes cannot see Allah, and to look at the mountain; if it remains in its place, Moses can see Allah." When Allah appeared on the mountain, Moses (Musa) passed out, unconscious, and the mountain was crushed down. After Moses aroused up, he said, "praise and gratitude are to Allah, the creator of the universe. I repent, and I am the first one who believed from the current children of Israel." According to the interpretation of Islamic resources, Allah, the creator of the universe, chose the prophet and messenger Moses (Musa) over the people of the world. Allah wrote the Torah to him on the tablets of stones. He ordered Moses (Musa) to take whatever Allah gave to him and to be grateful. And on the stone plaques, Allah wrote the Ten Commandments and the Torah. And Allah told Moses (Musa) to take the tablets from the stone plaques, with powerful faith, to the children of Israel. And Allah told him who were defiant from the children of Israel.

Alsamery

Alsamery misled the children of Israel and made a golden calf from their gold, and he told them to worship it. After the prophet Moses (Musa) left for forty days, the children of Israel made a calf statue from their gold jewelry. It had openings for air to be pushed through it, causing a low noise.

[Then he brought out (of the fire) before (the people) the image of a calf: it seemed to low: so, they said: "this is your god, and the god of Moses, but (Moses) had forgotten!"

Could they not see that it could not return them a word (for answer), and that it had no power either to harm them or to do them good? (The Quran Translation, Ali Yusuf 2007, 20:88-110)].

Those who worshipped the golden calf statue were extreme

sinners. They did not see that the calf could not speak to them or direct them to the straight way.

"My people, you are examined by Allah in your faith, but you worshipped a gold calf, and you stopped worshipping Allah. Allah is the most gracious. Follow me and obey my order," the prophet Aaron (Haroun) said to the children of Israel.

"We will not stop worshipping the golden calf statue until Moses returns to us," the children of Israel said to Aaron. The prophet and messenger Moses came back and was annoyed. He said to the children of Israel, "what you did was awful. Were you having intolerant about worshipping Allah?" The prophet Moses (Musa) put the stone tablets of the Ten Commandments to the side and then grasped his brother Aaron by the hair of his beard and head, dragging him.

"Son of my mother do not grasp me by my hair of my beard and head," Haroun (Aaron) said.

"When you watched the children of Israel going astray, what prohibited you from following my advice? Have you defied my order?" Moses asked Aaron.

"I have feared that you may say that I caused a partition among the children of Israel. I respected your word. The people intimidated me, and they wanted to kill me. Do not let the unbelievers get joy by putting me down. Do not count me among the sinners," Aaron replied.

"My people, you have destroyed yourselves by worshipping a golden calf. Repent to Allah," the prophet Moses (Musa) said to the children of Israel. And Moses (Mousa) burned the golden calf and threw it into the sea.

The prophet Moses (Musa) said to Alsamery, "in your life, there is no one to punish you, but your punishment will be on the Day of Resurrection."

[And remember you said: O Moses! we shall never believe in you until we see Allah manifestly, "but you were dazed with thunder and lightning even as you looked on. Then We raised you up after your death: you had the chance

to be grateful" (The Quran Translation, Ali, Yusuf 2007, 2:55–61)].

"We do not believe you until we watch Allah with our eyes," the children of Israel said to Moses.

A lethal thunderstorm took those party of the children of Israel, who died while they were looking up. After their death, Allah resurrected them. They might appreciate Allah. They knew that they had gone astray. The children of Israel said, "if Allah does not forgive us by mercy, we will be losers."

The prophet and messenger Moses said, "Allah, forgive me and my brother. And accept us into your mercy. You are the most merciful."

According to the Islamic resources, those who made the golden calf and worshipped it, angered Allah, and they were humiliated in the life of this world. Allah punished the makers of deception, but Allah forgave those who committed sins without intention and repented. He is the most merciful. Allah accepted the repentance of the children of Israel. He is the most merciful. Allah protected them with rain clouds and sent down sweet manna and quail birds.

And when the anger stopped, Moses took the stone tablets of commandments, which included guidance and mercy for those who feared Allah. Moses chose seventy men for an appointment with Allah, and an earthquake grabbed them. The prophet and messenger Moses prayed, "Allah, would you like to destroy me and those people? Do you want to destroy us for the act of the offenders among us? This was your trial. You direct whoever you want. You are our savior and are gracious. Allah, will you please direct us in this world and on the Day of Resurrection. We have turned to you."

The Grace

According to the interpretation of Islamic resources, Allah grants forgiveness for those who fear him, those who give charity to the needy, and those who believe in his words. Among the people of Moses (Musa), a community was led by truth and validated justice. Allah granted them compassion, and his grace comprises all his creatures.

The children of Israel asked Moses for water. The prophet and messenger Moses (Musa) prayed to Allah and asked for water. And Moses formed groups of the twelve tribes (Alasbat). According to the interpretation of Islamic resources, Allah ordered Moses to hit the rock with his rod, and water poured out from twelve springs. Every tribe knew their water spring.

The children of Israel said to the prophet Moses, "we cannot tolerate one kind of food. Ask Allah to grant us from the earth—green plants, lintel, garlic, and onions."

The prophet Moses said, "do you choose the less, rather than the valuable things? If you want the less, let you descend to Egypt. You will have whatever you ask. Remember, Allah saved you from pharaoh and his people. They were harming you with severe torture. They killed your sons and kept your women alive; that was devastating."

According to the interpretation of Islamic resources, the prophet Moses (Musa) said to the children of Israel, "Allah orders you to go to the holy village (Jerusalem) and eat whatever you want. Enter the gate of the village and prostrate yourselves. Allah will forgive your sins." They changed the words of Allah. Allah sent a plague from the skies because they defied.

[But the transgressors changed the word from that which had been given them; so, We sent on the transgressors a plague from heaven, for that they infringed (our command) repeatedly (The Quran Translation, Ali, Yusuf 2007, 2:59-60)].

The prophet Moses said "my people, keep in mind Allah's favors you, in appointing prophets among you, making you owners, and giving to you, which he did not give to anyone else in the world. My people, enter the holy village, which Allah has assigned to you, and do not turn back from fighting in Allah's cause."

The children of Israel said to Moses, "the holy village (Jerusalem) is occupied by powerful tyrannical people, and we will never enter it until they leave it."

Two faithful men said, "enter the gateway, prostrating yourselves to Allah. You will have victory. Trust Allah, if you are believers."

[They said: "O Moses! while they remain there, never shall we be able to enter, to the end of time. Go you and your Lord and fight you two, while we set here (and watch)" (The Quran Translation, Ali, Yusuf 2007, 5:24-26)].

"We will not enter this holy land ever—if those people are living there. Go, you and your Allah to fight. We are remaining right here to watch," the children of Israel said to the prophet Moses (Musa).

"Allah, the creator of the universe, I do not have authority except on myself and my brother Aaron (Haroun). The children of Israel are defiant," the prophet Moses said. According to the interpretation of Islamic resources, Allah told the prophet Moses (Musa) that he should not feel sad over the defiant people. The holy land was forbidden to the children of Israel for forty years. They wandered through the desert of Sinai.

The prophet Moses (Musa) said, "if you will not believe, Allah does not need anyone. He is self-sufficient. Keep in mind the favor of Allah upon you. He saved you from the pharaoh and his people. They were distressing you with the worst devastation. They were slaughtering your boys and keeping your girls alive, and that was great harm for you. If you are thankful, he will increase your earnings, but if you deny his favor, his punishment will be painful."

The Heifer

The prophet Moses (Musa) said, "Allah commands you to process the slaughtering of a heifer (cow)."

[And remember Moses said to his people: "Allah commands that you sacrifice a heifer." They said: "Do you make laughingstock to us?" He said, "May Allah save me from being an ignorant (fool)!" (The Quran Translation, Ali, Yusuf 2007, 2:67-79)].

"Are you make fun of us?" the children of Israel said to the prophet Moses.

"I seek the protection of Allah from ignorance," the prophet Moses said.

"Ask Allah to make the cow (heifer) visible to us. The cows have a similar shape," the children of Israel said.

"The cow is middle aged. Do what Allah has commanded you," the prophet Moses said.

"Ask Allah to show us its color," the children of Israel said.

"It is a deep-yellow cow which gratifies the eyes of those who see it," the prophet Moses said.

"Ask Allah to make it noticeable to us. Which is it? All cows look like each other. And if Allah wills, we will slaughter it," the children of Israel said to Moses.

"It is a cow neither trained for mowing nor irrigating the field. It is free from defects, with no spots on it," the prophet Moses said.

"Now you have come with the truth," the children of Israel said. The children of Israel slaughtered the cow, but they did not like to do it.

At that time, a man killed one of them. They were unsure over who was the killer. Then Allah let them to see the true justice that was concealed.

According to the interpretation of Islamic resources, Allah told Moses (Musa) to hit the man who was killed with part of the cow. Allah showed the children of Israel how Allah resurrects the dead. Moses showed them Allah's signs. The man awakened up and told them who had killed him. Allah saved the children of Israel from the humiliating devastation of the pharaoh, who was arrogant and dictators. Allah chose the children of Israel by acquaintance over all the world. He gave them signs and saved them from their enemy. They promised Allah, beside the right side of Mountain of Altor of Sinai, to be trustworthy believers. Allah sent sweet manna down to them and birds of quails and told them to eat as prescribed to them. Allah provided them free nourishment, but they should not eat excess. The punishment of Allah justly descended on the sinners. He is the forgiver to those who repented and believed, and they were moral—those who were ready to receive righteous direction. Allah sent Moses (Musa) with signs to move out the children of Israel from darkness to the light. The prophet Moses (Musa) reminded them of the days of Allah.

According to the interpretation of Islamic resources, Allah commanded them to worship Allah without association. And they should honor their parents, and they should behave morally with their relatives, orphans, and the needy. They should use justice, establish regular prayer, and they should give charity. They turned away, except a few of them, and they rejected the signs of Allah.

People of Sabbath (Saturday)

According to the interpretation of Islamic resources, Allah pardoned the children of Israel and gave Moses (Musa) a high authority. Allah raised the Mountain of Sinai over the children of Israel, they thought it will drop on them. And Allah commanded Moses (Musa) to tell the children of Israel to enter the gate of the holy land (Jerusalem), with morality and not to violate the Sabbath. And Allah took from them a firm promise. They caused Allah's anger by their defiance. They broke the promise and rejected the signs of Allah, and they killed prophets such as Jhon the Babtist (Yahya).

In a village, which was near the sea, the whales came on Saturday (Sabbath) to the people of the Sabbath (the group of the children of Israel), but the whales did not come on the rest of the days of the week. Allah gave the children of Israel a trial because some of them were defiant. They had transgressed in the matter of the Sabbath. Some of children of Israel said to the advisers, "why do you advise or warn those wrongdoers? They will be destroyed or punished with a painful torment from because they disobeyed Allah on Saturday (Sabbath). They put dividers in the sea to catch the whales."

The children of Israel who were obedient said, "we advise them, and they should fear Allah." The people of the Sabbath forgot what they were reminded. Allah saved those who did not use forbidden evil's works. He punished those who insisted on disobeying, with a critical punishment, because they were intentionally violating the commands of Allah.

[And you knew well those amongst you who transgressed in the matter of Sabbath: We said them: "Be apes, despised and rejected." "So, we made it an example to their own time and to their posterity, and a lesson to those who fear Allah" (The Quran Translation, Ali, Yusuf 2007, 2:65-66)].

Those who were defiant were disrespectful to what was forbidden. Allah punished the defiant of the children of Israel—they were turned to apes (monkeys). The Jewish people knew the story of those who transgressed among them in the Sabbath (Saturday). Allah made it a warning punishment for those who were defiant and to those who came after them, as well as a lesson for those who feared Allah.

According to the interpretation of Islamic resources, Allah knew what they had done. Those were people who preferred the life of this world in exchange for the eternal garden. The punishment would not be reduced for them. Allah took the promise of the children of Israel to follow the Torah and raised over them Altor mountain. Allah told them to take what he gave them of the Torah with powerful faith. And they should remember what was in the Torah; they should turn to the just. Then, many of them turned away after that without the support of Allah or forgiveness. And they were among the losers.

The King Talut (Saul)

The synopsis of the story of King Talut (peace on him) is according to the Islamic resources. After the prophet Moses (Musa) died, the next prophet said to the children of Israel, "Would you like to avoid war, if the war is commanded by Allah for you?"

"Why would we not fight in the cause of Allah, the creator of the worlds? We were pushed out of our houses, and our children were taken as hostages. We ask Allah to direct us, and we need a king. We will fight in the cause of Allah," the children of Israel said to their prophet.

[Their prophet said to them: "Allah has appointed Talut as a king over you." They said: "How can he exercise authority over us when we are better fitted than he to exercise authority, and he is not even gifted, with wealth in abundance?" He said: "Allah has chosen him above you. And has gifted him abundantly with knowledge and bodily prowess. Allah grants His authority to whom he pleases. Allah cares for all and he knows all things" (The Quran Translation, Ali, Yusuf, 2:247-256)].

"Allah chose Talut to be your king," the prophet said to the children of Israel.

"How will Talut be our king? We have supremacy over him to have the kingdom, and he is not rich," the group of children of Israel said to their prophet.

"Allah sent Talut to be a king. Talut had more wisdom and is larger in body. Allah grants authority to whomever he wills. Allah is gracious for his creatures and knows all. The sign of his kingdom will come to you, in peace and serenity. A holy box (Al-Tabut) will descend from the heavens. The box includes the holy book, the Torah, which was lost. The Torah was written on the tablets to the prophets Moses (Musa) and Aron (Haroun). The holy box will be carried by angels. This is evidence to the believers," the prophet said to the children of Israel. King Talut prepared an army and said, "Allah will examine you by a river. Who drinks from it will not be my follower, and who does not drink is my follower, except those who drink water just one cavity of his hand." The soldiers drank more water from the river, except a few of them, and some were dead. Then, King Talut crossed the river, as did those who believed in his message. Some of the children of Israel who were with Talut said, "we have no power against Galut (Goliath) and his soldiers," and they left the army. King Talut's army still had people who knew that they would meet Allah, some of them said, "A small group can overcome several groups of people with Allah's permission. Allah supports the one who has patience." The children of Israel prayed while they proceeded to meet Goliath (Galut) and his forces, saying, "Allah, give us tolerance, and

set our feet strong and grant us success over the unbelievers, Amen."
According to the Islamic resources, the King Talut was killed by his
enemy Goliath (Galut). Then, King David (Dawoud) killed his enemy
Goliath (Galut), and the children of Israel had the victory.

King David (Dawoud)

The synopsis of the story of the prophet and messenger David
(Dawoud), (peace on him), is according to the Islamic resources. The
children of Israel terrified their enemy in the holy land (Jerusalem), by
Allah's permission. And Allah empowered the king David (Dawoud)
to kill Goliath (Galut). Allah gave the prophet and messenger David
(Dawoud) the throne of the kingdom of the children of Israel after
the death of King Talut.

If Allah does not restrain a group of people from another group,
the earth will be full of transgression and exploitation. Allah is the
most gracious to the humans, jinn (unseen), angels and all creatures.
Allah granted strength to David (Dawoud). He often returned to
Allah in all matters and repented. Day and night, the mountains
worshipped and praised Allah with King David. The birds came
together in obedience to him. They worshipped and praised Allah
with him. Allah made David's kingdom strong and gave him wisdom,
the message, and judgment in decisions. Allah granted King David
the strength to shape the iron for making armors for battle to protect
him and the soldiers.

King David (Dawoud) had a son called Suleiman (Solomon). Both
judged people in conflicts. One day, two brothers had a conflict. They
climbed over the fence of King David's house, and they entered his
room; he feared.

"Do not be afraid, we are two men having a conflict. We want
you to judge us with justice and direct us to the straight path. My
brother owns ninety-nine sheep, and I own one sheep. He wants
to take my sheep," one of the two men said. Without listening to
the other man, King David said, "your brother has aggrieved you

by asking for your sheep to add it to his ninety-nine sheep. Many partners oppress one another, except those who believe in Allah, and they do good deeds, and they are few."

[O David! We did indeed make you a vicegerent on earth: so judge you between men in truth (and justice): nor follow you the lusts (of your heart), for they will mislead you from the Path of Allah: for those who wonder astray from the Path of Allah, is a Penalty grievous, for they forget the Day of Account (The Quran Translation, Ali, Yusuf 2007, 38:26-30)].

After that, king David recognized that Allah examined him, and he should listen to both men before judging. King David asked Allah for forgiveness, and he bowed down prostrated and turned to Allah in repentance. Allah forgave him and promised him the right place in paradise. Allah sent Al-Zabur book to the prophet David (Dawoud). Allah also sent a command for David to judge people in justice and that he should not follow his impression because it would delude him from the straight way. Allah made Solomon (Suleiman) to comprehend the case of the two brothers, and he judged with the right justice for them.

King Solomon (Suleiman)

The synopsis of the story of the king Suleiman (Solomon), (peace on him), is according to the Islamic resources. King Solomon (Suleiman) inherited the kingdom of his father. King Solomon (Suleiman) was a prophet of the children of Israel and a faithful slave to Allah. He often returned in repentance. Allah examined him and placed another man on his throne, he lost his kingdom for a while.

"Allah, forgive me and grant me a kingdom that no one can have it after me. You are the greatest giver," Solomon prayed.

Solomon repented to Allah and returned in compliance to his throne. Allah gave Solomon (Suleiman) his request; the wind ran by his order by Allah's permission. The unseen creatures, such as Satan (jinn) worked in front him, by permission of Allah. And if Satan (jinn) turned aside from

Allah's command, Allah burned the unseen jinn with intense fire. The jinn worked for King Solomon as he chosen. They made high rooms, designs, basins as large as reservoirs, and cooking containers. The unseen jinn were constructers and divers. The family of King David (Dawoud) worked with gratefulness. Allah granted treasures to Solomon (Suleiman) to spend or withhold. There were no limits for him on spending; he would not be asked why he spent. Angel messengers of Allah helped King Solomon (Suleiman), and he got a promise of the eternal garden as a reward from Allah on the Day of Resurrection. One day, King Solomon was watching well-trained horses fighting for the cause of Allah. King Solomon said, "I should not love these good horses instead of remembering Allah. The prayer should not be postponed, the dark of night started. It was Satan (evil) who made me, forgot. Bring those horses back to me." He wiped over the legs and the necks of the horses with his hand to take Satan out of them.

Allah gave King David (Dawoud) and King Solomon (Suleiman) knowledge. Allah sent to King David (Dawoud) the original Al-Zabur holy book, which denoted praising and appreciating Allah. And the virtuous people will inherit the lands of the earth. In King Solomon's army were groups of humans, jinn (unseen creatures), and birds. They stand in combat order, and they went forward. Allah granted him spring of copper.

"My people, King David and I were educated the language of birds, and we have given all things. This is a grace from Allah," King Solomon said.

[At length, when they came to a (lowly) valley of ants, one of the ants said: "O you ants, get into your habitations lest Solomon and his hosts crush you (under foot) without knowing it" (The Quran Translation, Ali, Yusuf 2007, 27:18-44)].

When they arrived at a valley of nests of ants, an ant said to the other ants, "enter your nest. King Solomon and his soldiers will damage you when they don't see you."

King Solomon laughed at the ant speech and said, "Allah gave me the power and ability to know the languages. Thank you, Allah, for the grace that you offered to me and my father, David (Dawoud). Please Allah, accept me and admit me, by your mercy, among your upright slaves. Where is the hoopoe bird? I do not see him. I will slaughter him if he does not bring me a reason."

The hoopoe bird came and spoke to King Solomon, "I have news, you did not hear before—I watched a lady in Sheba (Saba), where she is governing the people. She has been given the whole things that any leader on the earth could possess, and she has a wonderful throne. She and her people worship the sun instead of Allah. Satan (evil) has made Saba (Sheba) people love their sins and has barred them from Allah's straight way. They have not upright direction. They do not worship Allah."

"Allah knows the hidden in the heavens and the earth and everything in between, and he knows what you all say. Allah is the only divine. He has the supreme throne. We will find out if you tell the truth or lies. Give them my letter and come back, and I will see what they say," King Suleiman said to the hoopoe.

The queen of Sheba (Saba) received the letter and said, "my chiefs, this letter was delivered to me. It is from King Solomon (Suleiman). In the name of Allah, the most gracious, the most generous, you must not rank yourselves superior to me but come to me as believers who submit their faith to Allah. My chiefs: I want to know—what are your opinions?"

"We have a great nation, and we have a strong army, ready for wars, but the decision of the war is for you. Declare whatever you decide," the chiefs said.

"If the kings occupy a town, they will destroy it and make the most honorable people the bottommost. I will transport to him a gift to see what will happen," the queen of Sheba said. The ambassador of the queen of Sheba (Saba) went with the gift to King Solomon. King Solomon (Sulieman) said, "Allah provided me more than what you have. Enjoy your gift; take it back to your queen. We all will come to you with armies that you all cannot resist. We will drive you out from there, and you will be dishonored. My chiefs, who can bring me her throne, before they will come to me in obedience?" Solomon (Suleiman) said.

"I can bring it before you stand in your place. I am powerful and honest for such work," a strong Satan (jinn) told King Solomon.

"I can bring it while you blink your eyes," said a man who had knowledge from the holy book.

King Solomon found her throne placed before him by the man who deeply believed in Allah and had the knowledge of the holy book.

"This is by the grace of Allah to test me. I am grateful. Allah is rich and generous and does not need any of humans. My chief, go to change the shape of her throne. We will watch whether she will recognize her throne, or if she will be one of those who was not guided," King Solomon said. The queen came to King Solomon, and Solomon's chiefs asked her, "Is this your throne?"

"It is the same," the queen of Sheba (Saba) said.

"Allah gave knowledge to me before her, and I submitted my faith to Allah before her. She used to worship things besides Allah. She was one of unbelievers," King Solomon said.

"Enter the hall," they said to her. There was a glass surface with water underneath. When she watched it, she thought that it was a pool, and she raised her clothes, uncovering her legs.

"It is a glass surface with water underneath," King Solomon said to her.

"I have hurt myself. Now, I submit my faith to Allah, together with King Solomon. Allah exists, and he is the creator of the universe," the queen of Sheba (Saba) said. When King Solomon (Suleiman) died, no one told the jinn that Solomon (Suleiman) was dead except little worms of the earth, which slowly made holes in his rod. When his rod dropped down, the jinn knew that they did not know the future. After Solomon died, the rejecters from the children of Israel followed Satan's (evil) works of magic tricks. Solomon (Suleiman) was not an unbeliever, but Satan (evil) is an unbeliever.

[They followed what the evil ones gave out (falsely) against the power of Solomon: the blasphemers were, not Solomon, but the evil ones, teaching men magic, and (such things) as

**came down at Babylon to the angels Harut and Marot. But
neither of these taught anyone such things without saying:
"We are only for trial; so, do not blaspheme." They learned
from them the means to sow discord between man and
wife. But they could not thus harm anyone except by Allah's
permission, And the learned what harmed them, not what
profited them. And they knew that the buyer of (magic)
would have no share in the happiness of the hereafter. And
vile was the price for which they did sell their souls. If they
knew! (The Quran Translation, Ali, Yusuf 2007, 2:102)].**

Satan (evil) taught magic works and things that came to Babel,
Iraq, by the two angels, Harut, and Marot. The two angels taught
people the magic tricks, but they said, "we are a trial for you. Do not
be unbeliever by learning those magic tricks from us."

People learned from those angels how they caused separation
between the man and his wife, but they could not hurt any individual
without Allah's permission. People learned witchcraft, which harmed
them and did not help. And the user of magic tricks would not enter
paradise. How bad that they traded themselves, if only they had
known.

The Messenger Jonah (Yunes)

The synopsis of the story of the prophet Jonah (Yunes) (peace on him),
is according to the Islamic resources. The prophet and messenger
Jonah (Yunes) ran away to a sailing ship that was fully loaded. He
was like inmate running from captivity. He expressed anger and
disapproval toward his nation because they rejected to believe and
departed in anger. He imagined that no one could control him. The
sailing ship's sailors threw the prophet Jonah (Yunes) in the middle
of the sea because their ship was full.

**[Then the big fish swallowed him, and he had done acts
worthy of blame. Had it not been that he (repented and)
glorified Allah. He would certainly have remained inside the**

fish till the Day of Resurrection (The Quran translation, Ali, Yusuf 2007, 37:142-149)].

A huge whale swallowed Jonah (Yunes), and he wept inside the deep darkness in the abdomen of the huge whale. Then he said, "no God but Allah. Praise and glory to Allah, the creator of the universe, I was one of the transgressors. Allah, please forgive me."

Allah, the creator of the universe, listened to the prophet Jonah (Yunes) and relieved him from sadness. Allah saves those who have deep faith. If Jonah (Yunes) had not repented and had not glorified Allah, he might have remained inside the whale's abdomen until the Day of Resurrection. Allah's command made the whale throw up the prophet Jonah (Yunes).

Jonah (Yunes) was fallen out on a sandy beach, and he got sick. Allah planted a fruit tree (*yaqteen*) over the prophet Jonah (Yunes) as tool to alleviate his illness, but Allah is who cure and heal. Allah sent him a message to a hundred thousand people or more. The people of Jonah (Yunes) believed. Allah removed from them the penalty of their sins and let them have grace during their lives.

The Prophet Ezra (Uzair)

The synopsis of the story of the prophet Uzair, or Ezra (peace on him), is according to Islamic resources. The prophet Ezra (Uzair) was walking in a village that was destructed to its foundations, he said, "how will Allah, the creator of the universe, resurrect this village to life again?"

According to the interpretation of Islamic resources, Allah caused Ezra (Uzair) to die naturally for a hundred years. Then, he resurrected him to life again. Allah sent an angel who asked Ezra (Uzair), "how long were you dead?"

"'May be a day or a part of a day," Ezra (Uzair) said. And Allah sent an angel messenger to inform him Ezra (Uzair) that Ezra had dead for one hundred years. The angels said to him, "watch your food and your drink did not expire. Watch your donkey. Watch the bones—how Allah collects them together and cover it by alive body. Allah will make you a sign to the people." When this was shown clearly to Ezra (Uzair), he said, "I know that Allah, the creator of the universe, has the higher power and is capable over all things."

[The Jews call Uzair a son of Allah, and the Christian call Christ the son of Allah. That is saying from their mouth; (in this) they but imitate what the unbelievers of old used to say. Allah curse be on them: how they are deluded away from the Truth! (The Quran translation, Ali, Yusuf 2007, 9:30)].

After Ezra (Uzair) died again, the Jewish people said, "Ezra (Uzair) was the son of Allah, the creator of the universe." This was their statement by their tongues. They acted like the unbelievers. All praise is to Allah, the creator of the universe. Allah has no sons, has no daughters, and there is no one related to him.

The Prophet Zacharias (Zakariya)

The synopsis of the story of the prophet Zacharias (Zakariya), and Yahya (John the Baptist), according to the Islamic resources.

The prophet Zacharias (Zakariya) prayed and said, "praise to Allah. I fear that the people of my nation will miss the direction of the straight way. Please Allah, the creator of the universe, grant me a pure and blessed son, representing Jacob's (Yaqub's) family and me?"

Allah, the creator of the universe, listened to the prayer of the messenger Zacharias while he was standing in the chamber of prayer. The angels said to Zacharias (Zakariya) good news, "you would have a son, and his name would be Yahya. No one had that name before. John the Baptist (Yahya) would be a witness to the truth of the words of Allah. He would have good morals and he will be purified and a prophet, messenger of the words of truth, wisdom, justice, and values to the children of Israel. The prophet Zacharias asked the angels, "how will I have a son? I am an old man, and my wife is barren."

The angels brought information. "It is easy for Allah. He created you before when you were nothing. Allah does what he will."

Zacharias prayed and asked Allah, "will you please give me a sign."

Allah sent angels to the messenger Zacharias (Zakariya) to say, "the sign is that you will not talk for three days."

[So Zakariya came out to his people from his chamber: and he told them by signs to celebrate Allah's praises in morning and in the evening (The Quran Translation, Ali, Yusuf 2007, 19:11-15)].

Zacharias (Zakariya) went out of his prayer room to the children of Israel and said, "my people, praise and glorify Allah in the morning and night."

Allah cured Zachariya's wife. She and her husband did virtuous deeds, and they praised Allah with love and worshipped him. They got a son called Yahya (John the Baptist).

[To his son came the command: "O Yahya! take hold of the Book with might:" and We gave him Wisdom even as a youth. And pity (for all creatures) as from Us, and purity: he was devout. And kind to his parents and he was not overbearing or rebellious (The Quran Translation, Ali, Yusuf 2007, 19:12-15)].

Allah's commanded to the messenger Yahya to keep the holy book with powerful honesty. Allah gave John the Baptist (Yahya) wisdom, even when he was a youth. He was sincere and kind to his parents, and he was not domineering or defiant. Peace was on Yahya (John the Baptist) on the day he was born, the day he died, and the day he will be resurrected.

The Virgin Mary (Marium)

According to Islamic resources, The wife of Amran (Imran) said, while she was pregnant, "O Allah, the creator of the universe, I offer the child who is in my abdomen to your service. Will you please accept this child to be your servant? You listen and know all the matters."

After labor, she said, "I delivered a girl. You, Allah, knew that the male is not similar to the female. I chose the name Mariam (Mary) for her. I ask your protection from Satan (evil) for her and for her offspring."

According to Islamic resources, Allah accepted her prayer, and the

Virgin Mary (Mariam) grew in purity and grace. After the death of the Mary's father Amran (Imran), the prophet Zacharias (Zakariya) was assigned to be her guardian. Every time Zacharias entered her room, he found food: He asked her, "Mary, from where did you get this food?"

"Allah provides countless sustenance to whoever he wants," the Virgin Mary (Mariam) replied. The angels said to the Virgin Mary (Mariam), "Allah purified you and preferred you more than all the women of the worlds. Worship Allah sincerely, prostrate yourself, and bow down in prayer with the people who bow down to him."

The Messiah Jesus (Isa)

The synopsis of the story of the prophet and messenger Jesus (Isa) is according to Islamic resources. The Virgin Mary (Mariam) withdrew from her family to a place in the east of Jerusalem. She placed a screen to stay away from people for fasting.

Allah sent a chief angel Gabriel (Jabril) to the virgin Marium, and he appeared before her as a respectful man.

"I ask the protection of Allah from you. Do not come near me if you fear Allah," the Virgin Mary said.

"I am a messenger of Allah to announce to you the gift. Allah sent to you good news of a word from Him. Allah will create your son, the Messiah Isa (Jesus). He will be honored in this world and on the Day of Resurrection. Jesus (Isa) will be with those who are loved by Allah. He will speak to the people in his infancy and in his later life. Jesus (Isa) will be with the upright company," the angel Gabriel (Jabril) said.

"How will I have a son when there did not a man touch me?" the Virgin Mary (Mariam) asked.

"Allah creates whatever he wants: He commanded a plan; Allah says to anything, "**Be,**" and it is. It is easy for Allah to create Jesus (Isa) as a sign and a compassion for people. Allah will teach Jesus (Isa) the holy book of the Torah, wisdom, the commandments, and the holy gospel (Al-*Ingeel*). Allah will appoint Jesus (Isa) as a messenger and prophet to the children of Israel. And Jesus (Isa) will receive the real holy books," the angel Gabriel (Jabril) said.

[How shall I have a son, seeing that no man has touched me, and I am not unchaste? He said: "So (it will be): your Lord says, that is easy for Me: and (We wish) to appoint him as a sign to men and a Mercy from Us: it is a matter (so) decreed" (The Quran Translation, Ali, Yusuf 2007, 19:20-40)].

The Virgin Mary (Mariam) was the daughter of Amran (Imran), and she guarded her virginity. Allah sent the angel Gabriel (Jabril) to blow the spirit of the soul of Jesus (Isa) into her, and she was one of the devoted servants. She got pregnant, and she went to a remote place (Beit-Lahem) in a cave, high in large rock. The labor pain drove the Virgin Mary (Mariam) to the trunk of a palm tree. She cried in her pain and said, "Ah, I wish to die before this. I wish to be forgotten and out of sight."

A voice of the infant Jesus (Isa) called to her from underneath, "do not fear or feel sad. Allah created a stream of water under you. And shake the trunk of the palm tree; fresh dates will fall off. Eat and drink and please your eyes. If you see anyone, say, "today, I am fasting to Allah, the most gracious. I do not talk to any human." The Virgin Mary (Mariam) went to her family, carrying the infant Jesus (Isa) in her arms. Her family said, "Mary, you came with an incredible thing. Sister of Aaron (Haroun), your father was **not** a man of mischief, and your mother was **not** awful woman."

The Virgin Mary pointed her finger to her son, the Messiah Jesus (Isa).

"How can we talk to an infant in a crib?" her family asked.

[He said I am indeed a slave of Allah he has given me Revelation and made me a prophet" (The Quran Translation, Ali, Yusuf 2007, 19:30-40)].

According to the interpretation of Islamic resources, the infant Jesus (Isa) said, "I am a slave of Allah, the creator of the universe. He gave me the holy books and made me a messenger and prophet. He has made me blessed wherever I go. And Allah commanded me to keep regular prayer and charity throughout all my life. And Allah made me kind to my mother and not to be arrogant or terrible. Peace is on me the day I was born, the day that I will die, and the day that I will be resurrected." According to Islamic resources: the Messiah Jesus (Isa), the son of the Virgin Mary (Marium) was a word of truth with which many of the children of Israel disagreed. It was not appropriate for Allah to beget a son. Praise is to Allah. Jesus (Isa) was a human without a father, such as Adam was without a father. When Allah declares a miracle, he only says, "**Be**," and it is.

The prophet Messiah Jesus (Isa) grew a strong man and said to the children of Israel, "You all should serve Allah, the creator of the universe. This is the straight path. I have come to you with signs from Allah. I created from the clay of dust an image of a bird. I blow into it, and it turns into a bird by the permission of Allah. I heal the blind by the permission of Allah, and I heal the skin vitiligo by the permission of Allah. I resurrect the dead by the permission of Allah. And I will tell you whatever you will eat, and the things you have stored in your houses. These are visible signs if you believe. I came to you to confirm the heavenly holy books, which were sent before me. Allah permits you portions of what was forbidden. I came to you with clear signs. Fear Allah, obey me, and worship Allah, the creator of the universe, only. This is the straight way."

The Table Spread

According to Islamic resources, the parties from the children of Israel disagreed with each other. On the Day of Resurrection, Allah promised sorrow and a serious penalty to the sinners. Did they wait for the last hour of the Day of Resurrection to believe? It will come suddenly on all of them when they do not perceive.

When the Messiah Jesus (Isa) felt that there were deceivers in the children of Israel, he asked them, "who will be my followers (disciples) to the faith of Allah, the creator of the universe?"

"We are your followers (disciples). We believe Allah's signs. You, Jesus (Isa) bear witness that we are believers. We submit our faith to Allah only. We believe in whatever Allah has sent to you of the original gospel (Al-ingeel) and wisdom, and we follow you. We pray to Allah to write us with the witness of the words of truth," the followers (disciples) said.

Allah guided the disciples to have faith and to believe and obey the Messiah Jesus (Isa).

[And behold! The Disciples said: "O Jesus the son of Mary! can your Lord send down to us a table set (with viands) from heavens?" Said Jesus: "Fear Allah if you have faith" (The Quran Translation, Ali, Yusuf 2007, 5:111-115].

"Call Allah to command a table of food from the heaven for us," the disciples said to the Messiah Jesus (Isa).

"Fear Allah, if you are faithful," the Messiah Jesus (Isa) said. "We only wish to eat and reassure our hearts, to know that you have told us the truth. And we will be witnesses to this miracle," the disciples said.

"Praise to Allah, the creator of heavens, earth, and everything in between and the great sustainer. Please command to us from the heavens a table spread with food to be the first and last festival and a sign from your grace," the Messiah Jesus (Isa) prayed. Allah granted the table spread with food down to them. He warned them that if anyone turns to unbeliever, Allah will punish them with a penalty that no one had got before.

Glad Tiding

[And remember, Jesus, the son of Mary, said: "O Children of Israel! I am the Messenger of Allah (sent) to you, confirming the Law (which came) before me, and giving Glad Tiding of a Messenger to come after me, whose name shall be Ahmad." But when he came to them with Clear Signs, they said, "this evident sorcery (magic)" (The Quran Translation, Ali, Yusuf 2007, 61:6-7)].

The Messiah Jesus (Isa) said to the children of Israel, "I am a prophet and messenger of Allah. I was sent to you, confirming the commandments of Allah, the creator of the universe, which came before me. And I tell you the good news of a prophet who will come after me. His name will be Ahmad (Muhamad)." Ahmad or Muhamad has the same meaning in the Arabic language. When the prophet Muhamad (Ahmad) came with visible signs, the rejecters said, "This is pure magic."

There were two parties of the children of Israel—one party believed Jesus (Isa) and the other party did not believe. Allah empowered those who believed against the unbelievers, and the believers succeeded. He ordained compassion and empathy in the hearts of those who followed Jesus (Isa). Allah sent to Jesus (Isa) the original gospel (Al-Ingeel). Their priests devoted themselves to spiritual work. They designed for themselves a system; Allah did not propose it for them. According to the interpretation of Islamic resources, Allah commanded the people to seek genuine faith. He gave rewards to the children of Israel who believed, but some of them were defiant. Allah, the creator of the universe, sent the Messiah Jesus (Isa) as miracle to the children of Israel. The Messiah Jesus (Isa) will be an indication of the last hour of the Day of Resurrection.

The raising of Jesus (Isa)

Jesus (Isa) received information from Allah that Jesus (Isa) would be raised up to the heavens. Allah saved him from the torture of those unbelievers of the children of Israel. Allah would make those who followed Jesus (Isa) to be higher over the rejecters. The parties of the people of the holy books differed among themselves.

According to the Islamic resources, Allah promised sorrow to the rejecters in the upcoming Day of Resurrection. The rejecters of the faith of Jesus (Isa) put design and prearranged to kill Jesus (Isa), but Allah planned against them, he is the best planners. On the Day of Resurrection, all people will return to Allah. He will judge between them concerning the matters over which they argued. For those who believe and work virtuously, Allah will grant them rewards in full. He does not love those who commit major sins and those who refuse to repent. Everyone will come to Allah singly on the Day of Resurrection. Those who believe and are honest will be granted love.

[They rejected faith; that they uttered against Mary a grave false charge, and they said (in boast), "We killed Christ Jesus the son of Mary, the Messenger of Allah," but they did not kill him, nor crucified him, but so it was made to appear to them, and those who differ therein are full of doubts, with no certain knowledge, but only conjecture to follow, for of a surely they did not kill him: Nay, Allah raised him up unto Himself; and Allah is Exalted in Power Wise (The Quran Translation, Ali, Yusuf 2007, 4:156–159)].

The unbelievers of the children of Israel spoke against the Virgin Mary (Mariam) false speech. And they lied and said that they murdered the Messiah (Isa) Jesus, the son of the Virgin Mary (Mariam). In fact, they did not murder Jesus (Isa) or crucify him. It was an illusion to them, and those who differed had doubts; they did not have true knowledge. The unbelievers of the children of Israel made people lose the straight path.

The only fact is that no one killed the Messiah Jesus (Isa). Then, Allah raised Jesus (Isa) to the heavens. Allah is exalted in power and wise. On the Day of Resurrection, the Messiah Jesus (Isa) will be an eyewitness against those liars.

Allah will gather all the messengers, prophets together and ask, "what was the responses of the people to your teaching?"

They will say, "we do not know. You, Allah know all the hidden."

Allah sent the holy spirit (the angel Gabriel) to support Jesus (Isa). Jesus (Isa) talked to the people in the crib during infancy and in adulthood. Allah taught Jesus (Isa) the Torah, wisdom, the laws, and the gospel (Al-Ingeel). Jesus (Isa) made from the clay of the dust a statue of a bird, and he blew into it and turned the bird alive, by Allah's permission. Jesus (Isa) healed who was blind and who had vitiligo, by Allah's permission. And Jesus (Isa) resurrected a dead person, by Allah's permission. Allah restrained the rejecters of the children of Israel from harming the Messiah Jesus (Isa) when he exhibited the visible signs.

[The similitude of Jesus before Allah is as that of Adam;

He created him from dust, then said to him: "Be" and he was (The Quran Translation, Ali, Yusuf 2007, 3:59-60].

According to the interpretation of Islamic resources, Allah created Jesus (Isa) in the Virgin Mary (Mariam) such as he created Adam without father. Allah created Adam from clay of dust. And Allah said to Adam, "Be," and he was. The truth comes from Allah, the creator of the universe. The Christians of the holy book gospel (Al-Ingeel) should not cross the boundaries in their religion. The truth of the Messiah Jesus (Isa) is that he was not more than a human prophet and messenger and a word of decision from Allah, the creator of the universe. Allah sent the holy gospel (Al-Ingeel) to Jesus (Isa). Allah advised the Christians to believe all his messengers such as the messenger Muhamad.

Monotheism in Christianity

According to the Islamic resources, Allah raised the Messiah Jesus (Isa) to the heavens,

Allah asked the Messiah Jesus (Isa), "did you tell the believers to worship you and your mother, Mary (Marium)?"

[Never said I to them anything except what you did command me to say, to wit.

"Worship Allah, my Lord, and your Lord." And I was a witness over them whilst I dwelt amongst them; when You did take me up, You were the witness over them and you are the witness to all things (The Quran Translation, Ali, Yusuf 2007, 5:117)].

Jesus (Isa) said, "Praise is to Allah, the creator of the universe, I did not say what I had no permission to say. If I had said this, Allah, knew it. Allah knows what is in my mind, and I do not know what is in his knowledge. Allah, know all that is hidden. I said only what was commanded to say. I told them to worship Allah. I was a witness while I lived among them. Allah raised me to the heavens. Now, Allah is the observer and witness over them. Allah is a witness to all things. If Allah punishes them, they are his slaves, and if Allah forgives them, Allah, is exalted in power and is wise." According to Islamic resources, this is a day of the truth. The truthful people will have grants for their honesty. Their places will be in the eternal garden, with rivers flowing below their houses. Allah will grant them the gardens of delight. That is the great protector and fulfillment of all unforbidden desires. To Allah belong the kingdoms of the heavens and the earth. Allah has power over-all. On the Day of Resurrection, Allah will gather all together. Allah will ask all his messengers, "did you let my servants miss the straight way? Or did they choose to be away from the straightway by themselves?"

They will say, "we did only what you Majesty commanded us to do."

[They do blaspheme who say: "God (Allah) is Christ the son of Mary." But the Christ said: "O children of Israel worship God (Allah), my Lord and your Lord." Whoever join other gods with Allah, -Allah will forbid him the Garden, and the Fire will be his abode. There will be for the wrong doers no one to help (The Quran Translation, Ali, Yusuf 2007, 5:72)].

According to the Islamic resources, they surely have unbelief, those who say the Messiah Jesus (Isa) is Allah. Those who associate others with Allah, the creator of the universe, will not enter the eternal garden, and their shelter will be the hellfire. For those who commit unforgivable sins, there is not any savior.

[They do blaspheme who say: "God (Allah) is one of three in a Trinity:" for there is no god except one God (Allah). If they do not desist from their word (of blasphemy), verily a grievous penalty will befall the blasphemers among them (The Quran Translation, Ali, Yusuf 2007, 5:73)].

According to the Islamic resources, they surely have unbelief, those who say Allah is one of three (trinity). There is no other divine but Allah. If those people do not stop what they are saying, they will have a grievous penalty from Allah. Why do not the unbelievers turn to Allah and seek his forgiveness? He is a forgiver and most gracious. The Messiah Jesus (Isa) never said, "trinity." Allah is not parts. The people of the holy book should know that they have no power of Allah's mercy. The power is in Allah's hands only. He gives it to whomever he wants. Allah gives from his grace.

According to the Islamic resources, Allah warned the Christians that they should not say trinity. Allah has advised them to stop what they are saying, and they should say Allah, the creator of the universe, is an absolute one; praise is to Allah. He is exalted and has no begotten son. All the creatures in the heavens and earth will return to Allah. He is honored in all matters. The Messiah Jesus (Isa) never objected to being a slave of Allah, the creator of the universe. The angels are servants of Allah. Allah will gather all who are ignorant and all who are arrogant. On the Day of Resurrection, they will be gathered for the punishment of hellfire.

According to the Islamic resources, the Messiah Jesus (Isa) was no more than a messenger and prophet, such as other messengers and prophets who died before him. His mother, the Virgin Mary (Mariam) was a woman of authenticity. They consumed their daily food and walked. Allah made his signs visible to them. Now, see in what way the unbelievers are mistaken from the reality. They worship, besides Allah, something that has no power to harm or help them. Allah hears and knows all matters. The Messiah Jesus (Isa) said to the children of Israel, "worship Allah, the creator of the universe, only. Praise is to Allah; we did not take other protectors."

A party of the people of the holy book said, "the fire of hell will touch us for a few days."

According to Islamic resources, they made a mistake with their belief because of they formulated false narrative. How will they do when Allah collects all of them on the Day of Resurrection? There will be no hesitation when each soul will get Allah's decision, according to what he or she did. And they will have justice.

The Jewish said, "the prophet Ezra (Uzair) is a son of Allah" And the Christians said, "Jesus (Isa) is a son of Allah." According to Islamic resources, Jewish and Christians speeches are untruthful. They tell falsehoods and imitate the unbelievers in what they said before. Allah, the creator of the universe, sent punishment to the rejecters before them because they deluded the truth of an absolute one Allah. They take their priests and the prophets and messengers to be deity. The Christians pretend falsely and say, "the Messiah Jesus (Isa) is God (Allah)," they were commanded to worship the creator of the worlds. Jesus (Isa) was a messenger of Allah. There is no other divine. Allah is the only divine. Praise is to Allah. Allah has no partners; there is no one who shares the throne with Allah. They wanted to turn off the light of Allah with their speech, but Allah will not permit this. Allah's light continues, even if the rejecters hate that.

[O you who believe! There are indeed many among the priests and anchorites, who is on falsehood devour the substance of men and hinder them from the way of Allah. And there are those who bury gold and silver and do not spend it in the Way of Allah: announcement to them most grievous penalty, (The Quran Translation, Ali, Yusuf 2007, 9:34)].

According to Islamic resources, there are priests, rabbis, and ministers who use the wealth of people, but they do not use it for charity services. Some of them hide gold and silver, and they do not spend it in the cause of Allah. Announcement from the heavens to those priests, rabbis, and minsters: they will have a most grave penalty. On the Day of Resurrection, the heat of the fire of hell will be produced out of that wealth to burn their foreheads, their sides, and their backs. Those were the treasures that they buried for themselves. They will suffer the punishment of the hellfire. The people of the holy book argue about the prophet Ibrahim's (Abraham's) religion.

According to Islamic resources, the Torah and the gospel (Al-Ingeel) were sent after him. Do they not understand? They argue in matters that they know; why are they arguing about the issues that they do not know? Allah knows, and they do not know. Abraham (Ibrahim) was not a Jewish or a Christian, but he had true faith in Allah, the creator of the universe. He prostrated himself to Allah and submitted his faith to Allah, the creator of the universe. There was not a messenger or prophet said, "worship me rather than Allah." All the prophets and messengers said to their people, "worship Allah, the creator of the universe." Those who have taught the holy books, they have studied well that there was not any prophet or messenger who instructed people to worship angels or humans. Did the prophet and messenger suggest to them to unbelieve after they submitted their faith to Allah, the creator of the universe? Allah, the creator of the universe, sent the prophets and messengers to teach people to worship Allah. The Messiah Jesus (Isa) came with visible signs to the children of Israel, and he said, "I have come to you with the holy book gospel (Al-Ingeel) and wisdom and to make it easy for you in the points that you disagree. Fear Allah and obey me. You should have faithfulness to Allah; this is a straight path."

[In blasphemy indeed are those that say that God is the Christ the son of Mary. Say: "Who then has the least power against Allah, if his will were to destroy Christ the son of Mary, his Mother, and all-every one that is on the earth? For to Allah belongs the dominion of the heavens and the earth, and all that is between. He creates what He pleases. For Allah has power over all things" (The Quran Translation, Ali, Yusuf 2007, 5:17-18)].

According to the Islamic resources, they have certainly unbelieved those who say that Allah is the Messiah Jesus (Isa). Who can avoid Allah, the creator of the universe, if he has decided to destroy the Messiah Jesus (Isa) the son of the Virgin Mary (Marium), and his mother or everyone on the earth? To Allah belongs the higher power of the heavens, earth, and everything between them. Allah creates whatever he wants, and Allah is capable over all things.

The Jewish and the Christians said to the prophet Muhamad, "we are the children of Allah and are his beloved."

According to Islamic resources, why does Allah punish the Jewish and Christians for their sins? Jewish and Christians are human beings; Allah created them. He forgives who he chooses, and he punishes who he chooses. To Allah belongs the control of the heavens, earth, and everything in between, and to him is the end point. He sent down the original Torah; it was guidance and light. All the prophets and messengers submitted their faith to Allah. Jewish should judge by the Torah, which was assigned to them, such as the rabbis did in the past.

[We ordained for therein for them: "life for life, eye for eye, nose for nose, ear for ear, tooth for tooth, and wounds equal for equal." But if anyone remits retaliation by way of charity, it is an act of atonement for himself. And if any fail to judge by (the light of) what Allah has revealed, they are (no better than) wrong doers (the Quran Translation, Ali Yusuf 2007, 5:45–46)].

According to the interpretation of Islamic resources, Jewish should judge by the Torah, which was assigned to them, such as the rabbis did in the past. Allah advice denoted that people should not feel terrified of other people, but fear Allah, and do not try to change the Arabic Holy Quran for a price. Allah, the creator of the universe, commanded, the following laws to the children of Israel: the life is for the life, the eye is for the eye, the nose is for the nose, the ear is for the ear, the tooth is for the tooth, and the wounds are revenge. Whoever bounces his right as charity, it is a tribute for him or her. Those who did not judge of what Allah commanded, they were the transgressors.

According to the interpretation of Islamic resources, Allah sent the Messiah Jesus (Isa) the son of the Virgin Mary (Marium). Jesus (Isa) confirmed the holy books and confirmed what came before him in the Torah. Allah sent the gospel (Al-Ingeel) to the prophet Jesus (Isa). The gospel (Al-Ingeel) was knowledge and light that confirmed what was written in the Torah and as guidelines for justice. The Christians should judge by what Allah sent to them. Those who do not judge by what Allah sent are defiant. All appreciation to Allah, and peace on his people who he chose to be prophets and messengers. No one in the heavens and earth knows the future except Allah, and no one knows when the Day of Resurrection will be except Allah. Gratefulness be to Allah. He will show them his signs. They shall know, and Allah knows what they are doing.

CHAPTER 4

The Last prophet

THE SYNOPSIS OF THE STORY OF THE MESSENGER AND PROPHET Muhamad, (peace on him) is according to the Islamic resources. The ancient Arab tribes lived in Hejaz, Saudi Arabia. In Makah city, they worshipped Allah, the creator of the universe, such was the religion of the prophet Abraham (Ibrahim) and his son Ishmael (Ismail). In Makah, the prophets Abraham (Ibrahim) and Ishmael (Ismail) built the first house of Allah (temple), Al-Kabbah.

There was a king of Ethiopia and Yamen who wanted to destroy Al-Kabbah with his military. He sent his military; they were riding elephants. Allah destroyed the military of the elephants that their plot went away. Allah sent birds to throw hot baked stones from the hell of Seigel. And Allah made them like eaten stems.

[See you not how your Lord dealt with the Companions of the Elephant? Did He not make their treacherous plan go astray? And he sent against them flights of Birds, striking them with stones of baked clay. Then did He make them like an empty field of stalks and straw, (of which the corn) has been eaten up (The Quran Translation, Ali, Yusuf 2007, 105:1–5)].

Before Islam, a leader of Makah went to Syria for trading. In Syria, the people worshipped statues. The leader of Makah bought a statue of rocks, and he ordered the people of Makah to worship it.

The worshipping of statues spread throughout the Arab tribes. Then, the ancient Arab tribes changed their faith; they worshipped statues.

The messenger Muhamad was born in the third lunar month before 1,445 years ago. He was from the offspring of the prophet Ismail (Ishmael). The father of the prophet Muhamad was called Abdullah, and he died before Muhamad's birth. His grandfather took his custody because his mother was sick. She was called Amanah Wahab. His grandfather Abd-Almotalib sent Muhamad to a wet nurse (for breast milk) called Halima Alsadeia. The mother of the messenger Muhamad was ill and died when he was six years old. The messenger Muhamad lived with his grandfather until the age of eight years old. After his grandfather died, Muhamad lived with his uncle Abi-Talib, the brother of his father. The messenger Muhamad was raised as an orphan in his uncle's house. In winter, he went with his uncle to Yamen for trading, and in summer, they went to Syria for trading of food, clothes, and supplies.

At Makah, the lady Khadijah Khoiled hired the messenger Muhamad to trade for her. In summer, he went to Syria, and in winter, he went to Yamen. At that time, Khadijah was forty years old, and Muhamad was twenty-five years old. She loved his honesty and his good morals. Her servant asked him if he would like to marry Khadijah. Muhamad expressed his pleasure in marrying the lady, Khadijah.

They had been married for twenty years, and they had six children. The children were called Qassim, Abdullah, Zainab, Fatimah, Um-Kal-Thom, and Roqaia. The messenger Muhamad never worshipped statues. He was known to be of good morals, honest, and a decent man. He liked to go to a cave called Dar-Hera on Alnoor Mountain, two miles from Makah city. The prophet Muhamad worshipped Allah, the creator of the universe, as had his forefathers Ishmael (Ismail) and Abraham (Ibrahim) done.

The Angel Gabriel (Jabril)

On Ramadan, the ninth lunar month, at the mountain of Alnoor, the messenger Muhamad was sitting in the cave of Dar-Hera. The angel Gabriel (Jabril) brought the first chapter of the Holy Quran from Allah to the prophet Muhamad and said, "read in the name of Allah."

The messenger Muhamad was illiterate; he replied, "I cannot read."

The angel Gabriel said to him, "read in the name of Allah, the creator of the universe, Allah created the human from a blood clot." The angel Gabriel helped the prophet Muhamad to memorize the holy Quran.

[Read in the name of your Lord and Creator who created man out of a clot of congealed blood (The Quran Translation, Ali, Yusuf 2007, 96:1-2)].

Muhamad returned to his house, he was shivering, shaking, and feeling cold. He told his wife, Khadijah, to put a blanket over him and told her about the meeting with the angel Gabriel. She went with him to her cousin Warqa Nofal, a Christian minister. The prophet Muhamad told him the details of his meeting with the angel Gabriel (Jabril).

The Christian minister Warqa Nofal said, "Muhamad is the last promised messenger, prophet of Allah, the creator of the universe."

In the original gospel (Al-Ingeel), the last prophet, messenger's name was sent as Ahmad. The Messiah Jesus (Isa) said, "there will come a prophet of Allah, and his name will be Ahmad." In the Arabic language, Muhamad and Ahmad have the same meaning, which is thanking Allah. The messenger Muhamad memorized the holy Quran accurately, and he never added any word, and he told the people, the Quran as it is. The real speech (*hadith*) of the prophet Muhamad was clarification and interpretation. The messenger Muhamad's speech never contradicted anything with the Holy Quran. Allah keeps the Holy Quran to the last hour on the earth without change, but some current books of the prophet Muhamad's speech (hadith) may be not valid or reliable. So, the people should be sure that the current books of the prophet Muhamad's speech (hadith) are not fabricated by the enemy of Islam.

Invitation in Makah

The prophet and messenger Muhamad invited the people of Makah to worship Allah, the creator of the universe, but they should not associate with him. The first female believer was his wife, Khadijah. The first male believer was his friend, Abu-Baker El Sediq. The first youth believer was his cousin, Ali Ben Abi-Talib. The prophet Muhamad was forty years old when he received the first chapter number (96) of the Holy Quran. He was equipped with the Quran to debate with people.

At Makah village, during the pilgrimage committee meeting, the messenger Muhamad stood on Al-Safa Mountain, and he invited people of Makah city, "in the name of Allah, praise, and gratefulness. I am asking Allah's help. I am faithful to him. I declare no God but Allah, and I do not associate anything with Allah. People will die such as they sleep, and they will be resurrected, such as they wake up. They will have paradise forever or hell forever. Oh, people of Makah, protect yourselves from the fire of hell. In the religion of Islam, there is no difference between who is white or black, poor, or rich, Arabic or Persian, except in their deep faith to Allah. So, there is no difference except in fearing Allah. Oh, people of Makah, you worship statues, fire, stars, or other things. Those things which you worship cannot help or punish you. Those are images; you gave them names. Believe in the absolute one Allah, the creator of the universe, but do not associate with him. Our eyes cannot see Allah, but he watches all. People will die and become dust and bones. Then, they will be resurrected, including their forefathers. The time of the last hour is unknown to us and may come shortly." The prophet Muhamad was the messenger of Allah. He did not ask for a reward, and he did not want to be a leading candidate. He had patience with what the unbelievers said. He got the best knowledge from the holy Quran. The unbelievers of Makah did not accept the message and did not believe the unseen absolute one, Allah, the creator of the universe. The unbelievers spoke of backbiting Muhamad. The pilgrimage committee of the Quraysh tribes told lies to the people.

They said, "Muhamad was a magician and crazy, our statues make connections between us and Allah, and we will not stop worshipping them." The prophet Muhamad warned the people of Makah of a lethal thunderstorm, similar to the lightning and thunder overtook the Aad people and the Thamud people. He advised them to listen to the story of the prophet Hud (Houd), the brother of the Aad people. Hud warned his people in Al-ahqaf. He asked them to worship Allah, the creator of the universe, and not associate. Hud (Houd) said, "fear the punishment of Allah on the grievous day."

The prophet Muhamad advised them to believe that Allah gives life and death. He will gather all the people on the Day of Resurrection. There is no doubt, but most people do not know. He asked the rejecters in Makah to recognize that they were worshipping useless statues.

"Have the statues or other things you worship created anything on the earth? Have they shared anything in the heavens?" The prophet Muhamad asked, and he told them to bring the original holy books that Allah sent before the Quran or any remnant of knowledge that they had if they were telling the truth. They rejected the message of the prophet Muhamad and said, "our hearts are under covers and concealed from which Muhamad invited us to do. Our ears are deaf. Between Muhamad and us there is a barrier. Let Muhamad do his interests, and we will do our interests." The prophet Muhamad advised them, "Allah is the absolute one. I stand with the truth, and I ask forgiveness of Allah, the creator of the universe." And he warned of sorrow to those who associated with Allah in worshipping because they turned away from the straight path. The rejecters of Makah reacted in arrogance; they refused to believe that Allah is an absolute one, and they said to the messenger Muhamad, "this is our life only; we live and die. Show us a sign if you are truthful."

The Holy Quran's Miracles

There are scientific miracles in the Arabic holy Quran the following are selected of them:

1. The messenger Muhamad showed the people of Makah the signs (miracles) of Allah, the creator of the universe, such as that the moon split into two halves. The rejecters watched the miracle of the splitting of the moon. They denied and followed their feelings, but for every matter, there is a time of settlement.

   [The Hour (of Judgment) is near, and the moon is cleft asunder. But if they see a Sign, they turn away and say, "This is (but) transient magic." They reject (the warning), and follow their (own) lusts, but every matter has its appointed time (The Quran Translation, Ali, Yusuf 2007, 54:1-5)].

   The unbelievers of Makah watched the cleft in the moon, and they turned away and said, "this was visible magic. Our eyes saw the illusion of Muhamad's magic tricks." Nowadays, the scientists of space (astronomy scientists) discovered that there was an ancient cleft in the moon due to a split that happened in the moon hundreds of years ago.

2. Before 1,445 years ago, Allah, the creator of the universe, sent to the prophet Muhamad the holy Quran, which includes the information that Iron descend from the sky. The unbelievers did not consider that.

   [We sent aforetime: Our messenger with Clear Signs and sent down with them the Book: the Balance (of Right and Wrong), that men may stand forth in Justice; and We sent down Iron, in which is (material for) mighty war, as well as many benefits for mankind, that Allah may test who it is that will help, Unseen and His Messengers: For Allah is full strength, Exalted in Might (and able to enforce His will), (The Quran Translation, Ali, Yusuf 2007, 57:25)].

Iron is a valuable metal. Allah makes it evident to those who support his message and his messengers that he is the higher power and exalted. The scientists discovered that iron descend from the sky such as the of dust of inorganic iron which come through the winds, it is oxidized to Iron Oxide (Fe203).

3. There was a war between the secular Persians (ancient Iranians) and the Romans (ancient Christians). The rejecters in Makah wanted the secular Persians to have the victory, but the Muslims wanted the Roman Christians to have the victory.

    [A.L.M., the Roman Empire has been defeated-in a land close by; but they, (even) after (this) defeat of their, will soon be victorious. Within a few years. With Allah is the decision, in the past and in the future: on that Day shall be the Believers rejoice (The Quran Translation, Ali, Yusuf 2007, 30:1-5)].

    The prophet Muhamad got information from the Quran, and he told the rejecters before the victory that the Romans Christians were beaten and overwhelmed in the nearest land (Persia), but after their loss, they would have the victory. The unbelievers did not acknowledge that.

4. Before 1,445 years ago, there was not any study of geology to know that the earth's layers were formed of seven layers, but the Quran includes that information.

    [Allah is He who created Firmament (the skies) and the earth a similar number. Through the midst of them (all) descends His command: that you may know that Allah has power over all things, and that comprehend

all things in (His) knowledge (The Quran Translation, Ali, Yusuf 2007, 65:12)].

According to the Islamic resources, Allah created seven heavens and seven layers of the earth, and Allah's commands descended between them. The people should know that Allah has the higher power over all things; he is capable and has all knowledge. The unbelievers did not accept that.

5. The Quran includes information about the pharaoh. Allah saved the body of the pharaoh of Egypt, during the prophet and messenger Moses's time, as a sign to those who would live after him.

[(It was said to him): Ah now! - But a little while before, you were in rebellion! – and you did mischief (and violence)! This day shall We save you in your body, that you may be a Sign to those who come after you! But verily, many among mankind are heedless of our Signs! (The Quran Translation, Ali, Yusuf 2007, 10:91-93)]

Many humans disregarded Allah's signs. The mummy of the pharaoh was part of Moses's message, currently he is in the Ancient Egyptian exhibition. The rejecters did not believe that.

6. Before 1,445 years ago, Allah sent the miracles in the holy Quran, which was landed via the angel Gabriel (Jabril) to the prophet Muhamad. The Quran includes knowledge included in the current sciences of embryology, physiology, anatomy, and gerontology, etc. According to the Islamic resources, the signs of Allah are present in the creation of the first human from the dust of clay.

[We created Man from Quintessence of (clay); then we placed him as (a drop of) sperm in a place rest, firmly fixed. Then We made the sperm into a clot of coagulated blood; then of that clot We made a (fetus) lump; then We made of that lump bones and clothed the bones with flesh; then We developed out of another creature. So blessed be Allah, the best to create! After that, at length you will die. Again, on the Day of Judgment you will be raised up (The Quran Translation, Ali, Yusuf 2007, 23:12-17)].

Allah created the offspring of humans from microscopic elements (sperm) in a firm sac (testes). It ascends in the uterus of a mother to join with the ova to form a blood clot (as a zygote). Next, Allah creates from the blood clot an embryo's flesh. And he develops bones from the embryo's flesh and covers the bones with the human body. All the humans will die, and on the Day of Resurrection, they will wake up. Allah has created humans and gets them out (into the light) as an infant. He makes humans grow and reach full strength. He lets them live to old age, while the others die at early ages. All people live to their appointed terms that they should learn wisdom. If the people have doubts about the Day of Resurrection, Allah shows them his manifest power. The unbelievers did not care about that.

7. Before 1,445 years ago, the miraculous scientific information of astronomy was sent in the holy Quran from Allah to the prophet Muhamad. Do people know what Altariq is? Star causes sounds such as knocking. It is a piercing star.

    [By the sky and the Night-Visitant (therein); – And what will explain to you the Night Visitant is? (It is) the Star of piercing brightness (The Quran Translation, Ali, Yusuf 2007, 86:1-4)].

According to the Islamic resources, the sky includes a bright star called Altariq. The holy Quran includes information about the piercing bright star Altariq (night visitor star, which causes sounds like knocking). The rejecters denied that.

8. Before 1,445 years ago, no one knew that the atom's weight was the tiny weight in the molecule of the atomic mass. The Holy Quran includes information about the atom and atomic weight. Whoever made an atom's weight a good deed will have a reward for it, and whoever made an atom's weight an evil work will have punishment for it.

    [Then shall anyone who has done an atom's weight of good, shall see it! And anyone who has done an atom's weight of evil (act), shall see it (The Quran Translation, Ali, Yusuf 2007, 99:7-8)].

    In chemical and physical sciences, the molecule is formed of two atoms and electrons. In 1803, John Dalton discovered the atomic mass is the smallest weight. The unbelievers did not consider that.

9. Before 1.445 years ago, Allah sent the holy Quran to the prophet Muhamad. It includes information about the electromagnetic waves and centrifugal force (outward). A brief interpretation of the Islamic resources notes that Allah grasped the heavens and the earth and prevented them from moving out of their places.

    [He is Allah Who sustains the heavens and the earth, lest they cease (to function) and if they should fail, there is none -not one- can sustain them thereafter: verily He is the Most Forbearing, oft -Forgiving (The Quran Translation, Ali. Yusuf 2007, 35:41)].

Nowadays, physics and chemistry indicate that iron elements can have a positive electromagnetic charge or negative electromagnetic charge. The electromagnetic force keeps the negative and positive iron elements trapped, although the two positive centrifugal chargers of iron elements keep the particulars vast away. Allah created the heavens, earth, and everything in between. The world is surrounded by the atmospheric layer, which includes electromagnetic waves or fields, which help the steadiness of everything on the earth to keep it in its place. The electromagnetic waves of the earth keep the things steady on the earth, and the centrifugal force keeps the elements away vast according to Allah's will. The unbelievers did not want to identify that.

The Patience

The messenger Muhamad had patience and invited people to Islam, the religion of Allah. He remained on the straight way, according to Allah's command. He did not follow the desires of the rejecters. He has believed in what Allah has sent in the Holy Quran. He was commanded to ensure justice among people. The rejecters turned away, arrogant, and the prophet Muhamad continued advising them. The messenger Muhamad did not ask for a reward for this, except the love of relatives.

Allah will give the believers his wealth if anyone does worthy deeds. Allah is a forgiver and thankful. Allah sent advice to those who believe to forgive those who do not respect the days of Allah (the rejecters). He will give rewards to the people for what they earned. Allah is the owner of the heavens and earth, and the rejecters will lose on the Day of the Resurrection. The rejecters wanted the prophet Muhamad to leave his faith and worship their statues. The messenger Muhamad wondered, "why do the rejecters ridicule if they were reminded? And when they knew a sign, they mocked it. Allah will judge between his servants in those matters in which they have differed. The ungrateful people, when they had trouble, cried, and asked Allah to help them and turned in repentance. Once Allah gave them their favor, they forgot what they asked for and forgot what they prayed for, and they associated with Allah, the creator of the universe. Thus, they misled each other from Allah's straight way. The prophet Muhamad did his part. The rejecters refused to believe that Allah is an absolute one.

"We will not leave our statues to worship your Allah," the rejecters said to the prophet Muhamad.

The one who worships Allah, the creator of the universe, prostrates himself during the day and night. He or she stands in devotion and is careful about the Day of Resurrection. And he or she places hope on Allah's mercy; he or she is not equal to the one who does not. Those who understand, after they receive a warning from Allah, and those who reject the signs of Allah will never be equal. Those who feel fear from Allah's punishment will have great rewards because they had moral during their lives. The earth of Allah is wide. The servants of Allah patiently stick with the truth, and they will receive rewards without measure.

Human Rights

Human rights started when Allah sent instructions to the messenger Muhamad: to ensure the equal justice for humans, no matter their race, color, gender, age, economic status, or education. All people are offspring of Adam and his wife. No one is better than another, except those who have deep faith and are sincere to Allah. The holy Quran includes verses that stress equality and justice and forbid arrogance and racism. Allah created all humans from a man (Adam) and a woman (Adam's wife). They used reproduction with the permission of Allah. Allah made populations of countries and societies to know each other. The virtuous people are those who have deep faith in Allah. Allah has all knowledge and has all evidence. At the time of slavery, if the slaves converted to Islam, the rejecters of Makah put heavy stones on their slaves' backs. They put them in the hot desert, and they killed them by tying each leg to a running horse. Abu-Lahab was a hateful unbeliever. He was a brother of the father of the prophet Muhamad. He and his wife hated the prophet

Muhamad and harmed him. Abu-Lahab stroked lashes on the weak Muslims, forced them out of their houses, left them to starve, and prevented them from drinking water or fluids during the hot weather. The types of torture increased the depth of the Muslims' faith. Abu-Baker El-Sadiq and Othman ben Affan and other Muslims paid lot of money to free slaves who converted to Islam. Slavery was present in past centuries. Muslims have Islamic laws from Allah to free slaves in certain matters.

[Allah will not call you to account for what is futile in your oath but will call you to account for your deliberate oaths: for expiation, feed ten indigent persons, on a scale of the average for the food of your families; or clothe them; or give a slave his freedom. If that is beyond your means, fast for three days. That is the expiration of the oaths you have sworn. But keep to your oaths. Thus, Allah makes clear to you His Signs, that you may be grateful (The Quran translation, Ali, Yusuf 2007, 5:89)].

According to the interpretation of Islamic resources, Allah will not blame the people for what is unintentional in their speech. He blames them for what they intended if they gave an oath or swore by Allah's name in vain. For repentance, the Muslim should feed ten needy people from the food, he feeds or give them clothes or free a slave (at the time of slavery). If he or she cannot afford that, he or she should fast for three consecutive days to erase this sin. So, they should guard their oaths. And if a Muslim killed an innocent human with intention, it would be a life for a life. If a Muslim killed an innocent human without intention, he or she could repent from killing by freeing a slave (at the time of slavery) or fast for two consecutive months or recompense money to the victim's family. According to Islamic resources, there is a story of a man who said to his wife that her back was like his mother's back. The man should stay away from his wife. If he wanted to repent and to have a relationship with his wife, the penalty was freeing a slave (at time of slavery) before touching her again. If the man could not afford that, he should fast for two months consecutively before he made a marriage relationship with her. And if he was not able to fast, he should give sixty poor people, one good meal. That was for the people who believe in Allah and his messenger Muhamad. And the rejecters would have a painful penalty in their lifetime and on the Day of Resurrection. Allah has all the knowledge. During the messenger and prophet Muhamad's life, the Muslims paid money to free the slaves. So, Islam is against slavery. According to Islamic resources, people asked the prophet about wars. Jihad is a war in the cause of Allah to defend people and the homeland. Terrorism and war in vain are forbidden. The use of violence against peaceful people, killing innocent souls, and suicide are forbidden. There are no verses in the Quran indicating that any Muslim will have seventy-two virgin women in the eternal garden after jihad. There is a promise in the sacred scriptures for who is made righteous that he or she will have a purified spouse in the eternal garden. In Islam, there are rules for wars. The transgressions of weapons violate the human rights. People were instructed to worship Allah only and to treat their parents with kindness. If one or both parents reach an old age, the individual should not say words to them in annoyance and should not shout at them. The individual should talk gently, show empathy to them, and say, "please, Allah, grant them mercy because they took care of me while I was young." People should worship Allah and not associate with him. And they should be kind to their parents, relatives, orphans, the needy, the close neighbor, the distant neighbor, the trippers, and the servants. Allah does not love the arrogant.

The Woman in Islam

The Arabic holy Quran includes verses confirming women's rights. Allah granted justice to the women in the Quran. This justice helps any woman in her life and hereafter, such as the virtues of marriage, fair rights during divorce, beneficial laws to the widow, and the inheritance laws.

Islam ensures the dignity of the woman; it regulates the sexual relationship that it should be in marriage. And the marriage in Islam has to be between female human and male human. Both should fill a written agreement in the name of Allah includes identity information, a gift from the groom to the bride according to his wealth, and the signatures of both and the signatures of two witness.

The man is responsible for supporting his wife in expense of food, clothing and housing. If a man divorced a woman, both should count three months of separation commitment before she marries another man. The man should not force his wife to move out of his house. She should stay in his house, except in the case of adultery. After the three months of separation commitment, he should either make up with her, obeying the regulation of Allah, or leave her by good manner. Allah helps those to pass this problem and provides them with grace which is unexpected. If the divorced lady is pregnant, the separation commitment time must be extended until she delivers her infant. The man should give to her from his income and let her live in the same stander as his stander. He should pay for her until she delivers her infant. If she breastfeeds his infant, he should pay for her. The man should give her payment from his wealth.

[O prophet when you do divorce women, divorce them at their prescribed periods, and count (accurately) their prescribed periods: and fear Allah your Lord: and do not turn them out of their houses, nor shall they themselves leave, except in case they are guilty of some open lewdness, those are limits set by Allah: and any who transgress the limits set of Allah: does verily wrong his own soul: you do not know if perchance Allah will bring about thereafter some new situation (The Quran Translation, Ali, Yusuf 2007, 65:1-5)].

The believers in Allah, if a husband divorced his wife for the third time, he should not remarry her again, except if she married another man and gets a divorce unintentionally. Then, she can remarry the ex-husband who divorced her three time, after the three months of separation commitment. If she is pregnant, she should wait until she delivers. **[When the souls are sorted out (being joined like with like).**

When the female (infant) buried alive, is questioned for what crime she was killed. When the scrolls are laid open (The Quran Translation, Ali, Yusuf 2007, 81:7-12)].

Before Islam, many unbelievers had buried living infant girls in the ground. The reason was that they were worried that the girls might have a future sexual relationship without marriage. The unbeliever man, after the birth of a baby girl, his face turned darker, and he felt angry. He hid himself from people because he believed this was the worst news. The Quran includes information that killing of the female newborn is forbidden. The Muslim men in Arab tribes were the first men who obeyed Allah in keeping the life of infant girls.

The Quran includes instructions and management plans of a structured family system and strategic plans to solve a Muslim's family problems. Muslims can ask the academic Islamic professors (imams) how to fix their social and family problems. The individual can find tactics and techniques to manage his or her family relationships and can solve conflict.

People asked the messenger Muhamad for instructions concerning orphans.

According to the interpretation of Islamic resources, Allah instructed and reminded people concerning the orphan woman: if a man did not give an orphan woman the portion of wealth which was arranged to her, and he wanted to marry her, he should stand firm for justice and uprightness. He was advised to give her a portion of wealth. Allah watches and knows who are weak or oppressed.

Emigración to Habasha

In the fourth year from the beginning of Islam, the rejecters of Quraysh tribes at Makah discriminated against Muslims violently. They penalized and tortured their servants who became Muslims. At that time, Muslims hid their conversion because the unbelievers of Quraysh tribes tracked them. The transgression and hurtful behaviors of Quraysh tribes had reached the highest peak toward Muslims. In the fifth year of the beginning of Islam, a group of Muslims emigrated to Ethiopia (Habasha). The leader of the Muslim group was Othman Ben-Affan, and his wife was Roqaya, the daughter of the prophet Muhamad. On their trip, they used two sailing boats as rides. At that time, the Quraysh tribes sent two men with gifts to the king of Ethiopia (Habasha). The rejecters of Quraysh said to the king of Ethiopia, "force the emigrant Muslims to get out of your country."

"Why did you all emigrate here?" the king of Ethiopia (Habasha) asked the Muslim emigrants.

The Muslims' speaker said, "before converting to the religion of Islam, we were unaware of our behavior. We worshipped statues, dishonored our parents, and hurt our neighbors. The stronger hurt the weak people and committed forbidden sins. The messenger Muhamad invited us to the religion of Islam to worship Allah, the creator of the heavens, earth, and everything in between. The messenger Muhamad warned us to stop association with Allah. He followed the guidance of Allah and advised us to honor our parents, to be moral with our neighbors, to be moral with the weak people, not to use adultery, not to kill innocent people, not to tell lies, not to use the interest of mortgage, not to take the money of orphans, and not trick the balance. He advised us to pray five times per day. And he advised us to fast in Ramadan month and pay charity for poor people. The interpretation of what the Muslims' representer said, "the messenger Muhamad received the story of the Virgin Mary (Marium) and the Messiah Jesus (Isa). The father of the Virgin Mary was called Amran (Imran). He was a religious leader to the children of Israel. He was from the offspring of the prophets Jacob (Yaqub), Isaac (Isehaq), and Abraham (Ibrahim). After the death of Amran, Mary's family, members made a race by throwing their wooden pens on a lake to see who would have the honor of the floating pen. The prophet Zacharias (Zakariya) won the honor of the guardian the virgin Mary.

Every time Mary's guardian Zacharias went to check on her, he found food in her room; he asked her, "from where you got this food?"

The Virgin Mary (Marium) said, "this is from the grace of Allah, the creator of the heavens, earth, and everything in between."

The messenger Muhamad was guided by the words of Allah of the holy Quran. Quraysh tribes did not permit the invitation to Islam. They prevented the spread of the Islamic religion, and they tortured Muslims and killed them. The king of Ethiopia (Habasha) asked the Muslims' presenter to read verses of the Holy Quran. He read chapter 19 (Marium), which includes the story of the Messiah Jesus (Isa).

According to the interpretation of Islamic resources: one day, the virgin Mary (Marium) went to an eastern valley in Jerusalem, holy land. Allah, the creator of the universe sent his messenger the angel Gabriel (Jabril), (peace on him). He appeared to her as a respectful man and said, "I have good news. You will have a son. His name will be Jesus (Isa). He will be the prophet and messenger to the children of Israel."

The Virgin Mary (Marium) asked him, "how will I conceive a child when no man has touched me?"

The angel said, "it is simple for Allah to do that, He says for anything "Be", and it is."

The Virgin Mary (Marium) conceived the miracle of pregnancy without a man, and she stayed in an eastern place. At Bethlehem, the labor pain forced her to the trunk of a palm tree. She said, "Ah, I would like to die before this day."

She listened to a voice calling under her. The infant Jesus (Isa) said, "do not be afraid, and do not have sorrow. Shake the palm tree to eat date fruits, drink spring water, and bless your eyes. If you see anyone, tell him or her, "today, I am fasting to Allah, and I am not talking to a human."

The Virgin Mary went to her family, carrying the infant Jesus (Isa).

"Mary, you made something horrible. Sister of Haroun (Aaron), your father was not bad, and your mother was not sinful," Mary's family said.

Mariam (Mary) pointed to Jesus (Isa).

The family of the Virgin Mary asked her, "how can we talk to an infant in a crib?"

According to the interpretation of Islamic resources, the infant Jesus (Isa) said, "I am a slave of Allah, the creator of the heavens, earth, and everything in-between. He gave me the gospel (Al-Ingeel) and the Torah. He made me a prophet and messenger to the children of Israel. And Allah made me blessed wherever I go. And Allah commanded me to pray regularly and to give charity all my life. He made me kind to my mother. I am not a tyrant. And peace is on me—the day I was born, the day I will die, and the day I will be resurrected to the life again." The king of Ethiopia (Habasha) knew that there were similarities between Islam and Christianity. Subsequently, the king decided to keep the Muslim emigrants, and he sent back the gifts of the Quraysh tribes.

The Suffering of Muslims

The rejecters of Makah intensified transgressions against Muslims and tried different ways to stop the spread of Islam in and outside of Makah. They started to torture their servants who converted to Islam. Quraysh tribes changed their belief of the Monotheism religion of Abraham (Ibrahim) and Ishmael (Ismael) to polytheism. They rejected the faith of the prophet Muhamad.

The rejecters of Makah asked the prophet Muhamad, "why was not the Quran sent to a wealthy man? Why did not the prophet Muhamad have gold from the heavens?"

They refused to believe in the Day of Resurrection. The messenger Muhamad clarified that if the killer died before the trial, the victim had died without having justice. On the Day of Resurrection, the criminal would have punishment. He chose the house of Al-Arqam to meet with Muslims and to teach them. The messenger Muhamad had two caring uncles, Abi-Talib and Hamza. Both continued to support and defend him.

Quraysh tribes sent a committee to Abi-Talib, complaining of the prophet Muhamad. Abi-Talib talked with them nicely, but they told him that they had no patience to tolerate Muhamad anymore.

Abi-Talib said to the messenger Muhamad, "stop your activity of invitation to Islam."

The messenger Muhamad replied, "my uncle, if you put the sun on my right hand and the moon on my left hand to leave what I am doing, I am not going to stop. I invite people to worship Allah, the creator of the heavens, the earth, and everything in between. I do not associate with Allah anything, and I memorize the holy Quran and tell it to the people."

"Go and say whatever you want. I will never overcome you," Abi-Talib said.

At that time, Quraysh tribes worshipped statues from stones or clay and other things. The messenger Muhamad invited the people of Makah to worship Allah, the creator of the universe, but they got angry. The Quraysh tribes asked Abi-Talib to let them kill the prophet Muhamad, and they would give him another strong man to be his son. Abi-Talib refused their request. The Quraysh tribes continued to hurt the prophet Muhamad and the believers in Islam. The Muslims worship Allah, and they do not associate him with anything. Abi-Lahab (the father of the flame) was a hateful uncle of the messenger Muhamad. He threw rocks at the prophet Muhamad. Abi-Lahab and his wife put nails in the messenger Muhamad's way. Quraysh tribes got tired of Islam. They asked the prophet Muhamad to change the Quran.

The messenger Muhamad said, "Allah sent the Quran to me, with the angel Gabriel, and I will not change it."

Quraysh tribes asked the Jewish rabbis to tell them how could they verify the religion of Muhamad?

The Jewish rabbis told them to ask the prophet Muhamad about three things:

(1) What was the story of old centuries?
(2) Who was the man who went east and west?
(3) What is the soul?

The messenger Muhamad was equipped with the Holy Quran, which includes the stories of the old centuries. It was the story of the

Companions of the Cave. And the man was Zul-qarnain, who went to east and west. The soul is from Allah's Command.

The Consent of Quraish Tribes

The rejecters of Quraysh tribes united against Muslims. They wrote a consent and placed it on the wall of Al-Kabbah (the first temple in Makah). The consent included that they should not trade with Muslims; they should not marry Muslims; they should not speak to Muslims; and they should not live with Muslims. The rejecters increased the prices of food and wholesales. Then the consent was lost.

The Sad Year

Khadijah Khoiled, the beloved wife of the messenger Muhamad, died. She had reinforced the prophet Muhamad. Then, Abi-Talib, the uncle of Muhamad died. He was kind with the prophet Muhamad and supported him. Abi-Talib refused to convert to Islam, and the messenger Muhamad tried to guide him. The interpretation of Islamic resources noted that no one can guide who he loves, but Allah guides and chooses who will be guided. Allah is the knower of those who were guided.

Signs before the Day of Resurrection

The signs before the Day of Resurrection were revealed from Allah to the prophet Muhamad. According to the interpretation of the Islamic resources, these signs are the following: a creature will come from the earth (*dabah*); it will speak to the people who got the word of the torment against them. Smoke will come from the sky and affect vision and cause pain. Gog (Yagog) and Mog (Magog) will get loose from their barrier between the two mountains, and they will cause corruption on the earth. There will be severe earthquakes that will make the mountains like ruffled wool. The skies will turn red. The planet will be fallen and scattered, and the seas will be exploded like volcanoes. An angel will blow the trumpet. All who are in the heavens and earth will die except Allah. Then, a trumpet will be blown again by an angel. All creatures will be resurrected and will stand up. The people will be like scattered moths. The skies will roll, such as a notebook. Hellfire will be opened to the severe sinners who did not repent on time; its doors have nineteen angels. The people who will go to the hellfire will ask the angels to end their torment or to let them die. The angels will say, "it is the order of Allah that those will stay forever in the fire of hell." The promise of Allah is rewards of the eternal garden of delight to the faithful believers who obeyed the commandments of Allah and repented before their deaths by sufficient time.

Forgiveness

Most emotional distress is due to the feeling of injustice, inferiority, or being victimized by someone else. Muslims should not feel resentment or rage toward those who hurt them. They should ask Allah, during the feeling of guilt or shame, to forgive them. Muslims should forgive themselves and others, especially if justice took place. According to Islamic resources. Allah forgives those who repent and loves the people who forgive each other. Muslims should follow the guidance of Allah to the straight way of paradise. Faithful people should not mock others, may be others are better than them. Women should not mock other women. They may be better than them. Do not call each other rude names. Twisted is the name of misconduct after belief. Whoever does not ask forgiveness of Allah for the sins, he or she is one of wrongdoers. At day and night, faithful Muslims, should praise and remember Allah with gratefulness. Muslims should accomplish five pillars. First pillar—declarations of statements that there is no God but Allah, and Muhamad was a prophet and messenger of Allah. Second pillar—Muslims should pray five times per day: at dawn (before the sun rise), noon, afternoon, evening (after the sun set), and night. The Muslim should purify his or her body with water (shower) specially after sexual marriage relation and after menstrual cycle. Then before prayers, Muslims should wipe, with water in hand (three times), on the face, on fingers to elbows, on the head, and on the feet to the ankles. Third pillar—fast in the ninth lunar month (Ramadan) and pay charity of Ramadan, which is a meal or its price to a poor person. Fourth pillar—annually pay charity from their reserved money, reserved gold, treasures, and harvests. Fifth pillar—visit the holy land of Makah if they can and Arafat. It is advised for Muslims to give a slaughtered sheep or cow as sacrifice on a pilgrimage feast. In the Hegari (lunar) year, Muslims have two festival celebrations: Al-fitter feast after Ramadan, and Al-Adha feast after Arafat Day of the pilgrimage. Muslims believe that Islam is not the reason for a tragedy, but it is a reason to terminate irrational thinking and to behave peacefully. The prophet Muhamad was guided by Allah. He used a system to direct humanity. Islam ended the worshipping of statues in Makah. Muslims invited the Arabs, who worshipped idols or statues, to worship Allah (the creator of the universe). During distress, the Quran helped Muslims to have patience and courage. The messenger Muhamad continued to teach Muslims how they can be faithful to Allah and how they can clear their hearts of hate and envy. The prophet Muhamad's speech helps Muslims to correct their irrational thinking and behavior. In Islam, the forbidden behaviors are the following: association in worshipping Allah, gossip, hypocritical acts, killing innocents, theft, drinking alcohol, eating pig meat (pork), having sexual relations without marriage, gambling, taking the interest of a mortgage, defraud balance, pornography, transgender sexual relations, lying, and committing adultery.

When Allah gives people a trial, such as loss of money, illness, or loss of loved ones, Muslims should have patience. They should ask Allah directly to help them in their tough times without a mediator and without communion. Thinking in the eternal garden empowers spirituality and motivation. In the holy Quran, verses include descriptions of paradise or the garden of delight. Allah, the creator of the universe, gives equal opportunity to all humans and the unseen to win places in the eternal garden. The faithful Muslims will win residence in the eternal garden.

According to Islamic resources, the messenger Muhamad advised people to correct the maladaptive behaviors peacefully. They can defend themselves by using their manual defenders. Muslims should use speech to reject immoral behavior. If they cannot use their speech, they can use their thinking to refuse terrible behaviors. The messenger Muhamad also advised people to overcome doing sins and to stop forbidden behaviors. Muslims should not love substances. The Quran has information that refers to how they can pass from the darkness of sins to the light of the upright. The messenger Muhamad advised Muslims to love Allah more than anything and to screen their mistakes, and to stop conflicts between each other. They should respect their belief and should not defraud the products while they are using the counterbalance. They should be honest and ensure justice and equality.

Emigration to Yathrib

There were severe conflicts and violence from Quraysh tribes against Muslims. The rejecters of Makah knew that the messenger Muhamad would migrate, and the religion of Islam would spread around Makah. The second emigration of Muslims was from Makah city to Yathrib city (Al-Medina Al-Munawara). A group of men and their families emigrated from Makah. The unbelievers of Makah collected forty strong men from Quraysh tribes and other tribes. They gave them long sharp knives to kill the prophet Muhamad. The leaders of Makah said, "surround Muhamad's house and wait until late at night, when Muhamad will go to pray at the dawn, kill him."

[Yasin. By the Quran full of wisdom, you are indeed one of the messengers on a straight way. It is a Revelation sent down by (Him), the Exalted in Might, Most Merciful. In order that you may admonish a people, whose fathers had received no admonition, and who therefore remain heedless (of the signs of Allah). The Word is proved true against the greater part of them: for they do not believe. We have put Yokes

round their necks right up to their chins, so that their heads are forced up (and they cannot see). And We have covered them up; so, they cannot see (The Quran Translation, Ali, Yusuf 2007, 36:1-10)].

The forty-armed men of Arab tribes surrounded the messenger Muhamad's house. At that time, his cousin Ali Ben Abi-Talib was visiting him. His cousin Ali took a nap in the house of the prophet Muhamad. The messenger Muhamad went outdoors among the forty-armed strong men. Allah's miracle made, the necks of those armed men were locked, and their eyes were covered by a screen-like fog.

The messenger Muhamad passed between them, and they did not see him. He walked with his friend toward Yathrib city. The rejecters entered the house with their long sharp knives to kill the messenger Muhamad, but they did not find him. The rejecters of Makah followed in his footsteps, and they ran after him toward Yathrib city. He and his friend hid in a cave in Altor Mountain. The rejecters did not see them.

The other miracles were the following: a bird incubating her eggs above the cave and a spider's web closed the opening of the cave.

His friend said, "if they look down, they will see us."

The prophet Muhamad said to his friend, "do not be afraid, Allah is with us."

After the rejecters went away, the prophet Muhamad and his friend Abu Baker El-Sediq continued their way to Yathrib (Al-medina Al-Munawara). They used camels from the desert to travel. The distance from Makah to Yathrib city is almost 227 miles. Yathrib city residents were waiting for the prophet Muhamad, and they welcomed the messenger Muhamad with a song of Albader. The messenger Muhamad built the first mosque the location that his camel sat down.

The Hypocrites

The hypocrites of Yathrib (Al-medina Al- Munawara) and the rejecters of Makah city united against the Muslims. They initiated wars in the Bader Battle, the Uhud Mountain Battle, and the Alkhandaq

Battle. Allah sent angels to support Muslims during the wars. After this sadness, Allah sent down serenity on the faithful Muslims, but hypocrites worried about themselves, thinking of Allah as other than the truth.

The hypocrites of Muslims said, "is there anything for us to do in this decision of fighting in the cause of Allah? If we had anything to do with the decision of fighting, our people would not have been killed."

[Those who were left behind (in the Tabuk expedition) rejoiced in their interaction behind the back of the Messenger of Allah: they hated to strive and fight, with their goods and their persons, in the cause of Allah: they said, "go not forth in the heat." Say, "the fire of hell is fiercer in heat." If only they could understand (The Quran Translation, Ali, Yusuf 2007, 9:81)].

All the decisions belong to Allah. The hypocrites hid in their minds what they did not reveal. Even if they stayed in their houses, for those to whom death was commanded, the death would go to their beds. Allah tested what was in people's minds and purified what was in their hearts. Allah knew well their secrets. The messenger Muhamad had patience with what the rejecters proclaimed, and he stepped away from them in a respectable manner.

When a single tragedy attacked the Muslims in the Uhud battle, although they had victory twice in Bader and Hanine battels, the hypocrites said, "from where this loss of the Uhud Battel is?" The loss in the Uhud Battle was from themselves because they went to collect their winnings of the war and left their spots in the army during the fighting with their enemies. Allah is capable overall. The hypocrites said to their brothers, "stay at home," and when their brothers were killed, they said, "if our brothers had obeyed us, they would not have been killed."

They could not escape from death. Did the Muslims see the hypocrites establish regular prayers and spend regular charity? When the order of Allah for fighting was issued to them, a group of them feared people even more than they should have feared Allah. The hypocrites asked Allah, "why did you order us to fight? Would you not grant us a respite in our lives?"

According to Islamic resources, the gratification of this world is short. The garden of delight is the best for those who act virtuously. All people will have justice. Wherever the people are, the death will find them, even if they are in strong high towers which they were built up.

If good things befall the hypocrites, they say, "This is from Allah." And if trouble occurs, they say, "this is from the messenger Muhamad." The hypocrites were defiant and disputed with prophet Muhamad. According to Islamic resources, if people love their parents, their children, their brothers, their mates, their allies, their wealth that they have gained, the trade that they fear to decline, or the houses in which they have joy more than Allah and his messenger (Muhamad) or more than striving in the cause of Allah, they should wait, Allah will bring his penalty. He does not guide the defiant. Nothing will happen to the people except what Allah has decided for them. Allah is their protector, and Muslims should put their trust in Allah.

The hypocrites can expect one of two things for faithful Muslims: death in the cause of Allah or victory over their enemy. And Muslims can expect for the hypocrites either direct punishment from Allah or Allah's order to punish them by the Muslims' hands. So, they wait, and the Muslims wait too. If the hypocrites spend charity for the cause of Allah, willingly or unwilling; Allah will not accept their charity because they are defiant people. The hypocrites presented their excuses to the messenger Muhamad when he returned to them, and they apologized. Muslims should not believe them. Allah sent in the holy Quran verses concerning the hypocrites 'falsehoods. Allah knew their lies. If they behaved morally, Allah would observe their behavior, and his messenger, and the believers. They would be returned to Allah, the knower of what was hidden and what was disclosed. He would show them their wrongdoers. If they turned away, there is no divine but Allah. Allah is the highest on the throne of glory. Nothing will happen for us except what Allah decided for us. He is our rescuer, and the believers depend on Him.

The hypocrites of Yathrib city rejected to fight, in the Alahzab Battle and said, "our houses are exposed to harm."

According to Islamic resources, Running away would not help the hypocrites if they were running away from death or killing. The hypocrites crawled during the war and said, "whenever the prophet Muhamad is ready to march and take a decision of war, we will follow him." The hypocrites wished to change Allah's word in the Quran. They would not follow the prophet Muhamad. Allah has already said this before.

The hypocrites said, Muhamad is jealous of us. We were only talking carelessly and playfully.

According to Islamic resources: were the hypocrite's people cunning with Allah and his signs and his messengers? Who are those who lose their virtuous deeds? Those who have worldly life, while they think that they are doing moral deeds. Those do not believe in the words of Allah, the creator of the universe, and they do not believe in the Day of Resurrection. So, their deeds have become worthless, and Allah will not look at them on the Day of Resurrection. Their penalty will be the fire of hell because they denied it. They mocked Allah's signs and the messengers of Allah. Those who have believed and did good deeds will live in the higher garden of Al-Ferdous as a housing forever. If the ocean were fluid of ink to write the words of Allah, the ocean would run dry before the words of Allah, even if they added another ocean of liquid ink. The desert's Arabs said to the prophet Muhamad, "we have deep faith in Islam." They were Muslims, but they did not have deep faith because they stayed behind. They had an order to fight against people of violent. They did not show obedience to Allah and to the prophet Muhamad. If they were obedient, Allah would grant them good rewards. Allah would punish them with a grievous penalty because they turned their back to the instructions of the prophet Muhamad.

Many people do sins while Allah outspreads the cord of mercy to them until they see the warning of the promised punishment of the last hour on the Day of Resurrection. They will realize who has the worst position and weaker soldiers.

Allah is the higher king of the worlds. The prophet Muhamad did not rush with the Quran before its verses were completed, and he asked Allah to enhance his knowledge. He has patience with what they said. The prophet Muhamad praised and glorified Allah, before the rising of the sun, before the sunset, during the hours of the night, and during the sides of the day that he was blessed. Muslims were waiting, and the rejecters were waiting. They should know who was on the straightway or who had received direction. The prophet Muhamad warned them, but the deaf did not hear the calls when they were warned.

People of the Holy Book

The Jewish debated with the prophet Muhamad. They said to him, "we believe in what was sent down to us, and we reject any other messages."

[And remember We took your covenant, and We raised above you (the towering height) of Mount of (Sinai) saying "Hold firmly in what We have given you and hearken (to the Law):" **they said: "We hear, and we disobey": and they had to drink into their hearts of (the taint) of the calf because of their faithlessness. Say: "vile indeed are behest of your faith if you have any faith" (The Quran Translation, Ali, Yusuf 2007, 2:93)].**

The prophet Moses brought visible proof to the people of the book. They took a gold calf for worshipping while they were sinners. Allah took their promise, and raised over them the mountain to let them take what he gave them with strong faith. People of the holy book said to the prophet Muhamad, "our hearts are wrapped and sealed. We cannot accept your message of the holy Quran, and we do not need any more messages."

According to the interpretation of Islamic resources. Allah placed cover on the hearts of the people of the holy book because of their defiance. Few of them believed it; they rejected the faith of Allah. The hearts of the people of the holy book absorbed the worshipping of the gold calf because of their defiance. How useless was that to which their faith directed them? If the eternal garden of Allah will be for them especially, and not for anyone else, they could seek death if they were truthful. They never wished death because of what their hands had made. Allah knows those sinners, who are enemies to the angel Gabriel (Jabril) because he brought the holy Quran to the messenger Muhamad by Allah's permission. The holy Quran is confirmation of what is in the hands of the people of holy book, guidance, and glad tidings for those who believe. Whoever is an enemy to Allah and his messengers and his angels Gabriel (Jabril) and Michael, Allah is an enemy to those unbelievers. The children of Israel said to the prophet Muhamad, "Allah ordered us that we should not believe any messenger unless he showed us a sacrifice consumed by a holy fire from the heavens."

According to Islamic resources, there were messengers and prophets of Allah who came with visible signs for the children of Israel, even those prophets who got the holy fire to burn the sacrifice. They killed prophets such as Jhon the Babtist (Yahya). And many of them rejected to believe Jesus (Isa). They promised Allah to make their holy book (Torah) known and familiar to the world and not to hid it. They threw Torah away behind their backs and purchased little gain, that was a horrible deal that they bought. They displaced the words of Allah from the correct places. They said that they heard, but they disobeyed. It would have been better for the people of the holy book if they said, "we hear and we obey. Will you please, Allah, hear us and look at us?" Allah has cursed the defiant people. They did not submit their faith to Allah, the creator of the universe, except a few of them.

[Those who reject (Truth) among the People of the Book and among the Polytheist were not going to depart (from their ways) until there should come to them Clear Evidence.

A messenger from Allah, rehearsing scripture kept pure and holy. Wherein are laws (or decrees) right and straight. Nor did the People of the Book make schisms, until after there came to them Clear Evidence. And they have been commanded no more than this to worship Allah, offering Him sincere devotion, being True (in faith) to establish regular Prayer and to practice regular Charity, and that is the Religion Right and Straight. Those who reject (Truth) among the People of the Book and among the Polytheists will be in the hellfire, to dwell therein forever. they are the worst of creature (The Quran Translation, Ali, Yusuf 2007, 98:1-8)].

According to Islamic resources, the individual who knew the commandments of Allah in the Torah and did not follow it, such as the donkey who carries bulk. Worthless is the human who reject Allah's signs. And Allah does not guide the transgressors. Why did they kill messengers and prophets of Allah, the creator of the universe, if they spoke the truth? The messenger Muhamad conveyed to them the Arabic holy Quran. They were ordered to worship Allah, the creator of the universe, and to pray regularly and to donate to charity, which is the upright way. Those rejecters from the holy book believers and the nonspiritual will remain in the hellfire forever. Those are the wickedest people. According to the interpretation of Islamic resources, Allah warned the children of Israel that they will cause corruption on the earth twice, and they will have higher standers. When the first promise of Allah will occur, Allah will send his servants of great power against them, who will destroy their inner homes, this will be a mission. Then, Allah will give the children of Israel the upper hand over their enemy and will aid them with wealth and sons, causing increase in their numbers. If they direct themselves rightly, it was for their own selves, but if they acted mischievously, it was for their own selves. When the second promise of Allah will happen, before the Day of Resurrection, their enemy will humiliate them and harm their faces. And their enemy will enter the mosque of Al-Aqsa, in Jerusalem, as they entered it, in the first time, saying

Allah the greatest and they will destroy whatever was elevated. Allah will grant mercy to the children of Israel if they repent, but if they return to sins, Allah will send back the punishment to them. Allah constructed the fire of hell for the unbelievers. The prophet Muhamad did not let the rejecters cause sadness to him. Those hurried before each other in wickedness, among those who said that they believed with their mouths, but their hearts did not have faith, and among the Jewish who listened to any invention, and they listened to others who never came to the prophet and messenger Muhamad. The people of the holy book (Jewish) told the prophet Muhamad to bring down a holy book from the heavens. They asked the prophet Moses (Musa) more than this—they asked him to show them Allah, the creator of the universe. A lethal thunderstorm hit them for their sins. They took the gold calf for worshipping after clear evidence had come to them.

According to the Islamic resources, the people of the holy book made assumptions. Among the people of the holy book are those who are illiterate and do not know the sacred scripture. The children of Israel's hearts became tough, like the rocks or even harder. There are rocks from which the rivers gush out, and there are rocks from which the springs flow out, and there are rocks that fall, fearing the power of Allah. Allah is aware of what they make. And Allah knows what they hid and what they unveil. Allah promised agony to those who wrote a book with their hands and pretended that it was from Allah to earn money. Allah promised penalties to those for what their hands had written and sadness to them for what they deserved.

The people of the holy book said, "if we find similar verses in the Quran, as which we have in our holy book we take it, but if not, we should be aware."

According to the interpretation of Islamic resources, Allah did not want the unbelievers to get rid of impurities in their hearts. Allah promised them scandal and penalty in their lives and the afterlife. The people who were guided by the original Judaism thought that they were the best believers of Allah. They should express their wish for death if they were truthful. They would never wish death because of what their hands had done. Allah knows those sinners. The death from which they escape will meet them, and they will return to Allah, the knower of unseen. He will tell them the truth of what they have done.

"The fire will touch us for few days," the people of the holy book said to the prophet Muhamad.

According to the interpretation of Islamic resources, did the people of the holy book get a promise from Allah that he would not break His promise, or did they say of Allah that they never knew? The prophet Muhamad had an order to tell the people about the story of this man; and people should think about it: a man listened to the Quran, but he detached himself from its signs. Allah empowered him to be with the virtuous people, but the man preferred to stay on the earth with the sinners. The man followed evil works. He became like a dog. If you force out the dog, spread out his tongue, and if you leave him, spread out his tongue. This man rejected the signs of Allah.

Monotheism in Islam

Monotheism means that Allah is an absolute one. The prophet Muhamad got an order to worship Allah, the creator of the universe and not to join partners with him. According to the interpretation of Islamic resources, Allah's light is the illumination of the heavens and the earth. An example of his illumination is like a bright lantern. The lantern is inside a glass. The glass, as if it is a radiant shining star, the starts' light from the oil of a blessed olive tree. It is not from east or west; its oil would be luminous, even if it was untouched by fire—bright light upon bright light. Allah directs his brightness of light to whom he wills. He revealed examples for the people. Allah is the knower of all matters.

The Arabic holy Quran translation to English, chapter 112: "Say: He is Allah, an absolute one. He does not deliver. He was not born, and there is no one who is related to him." "There is no God except Allah—everlasting, self-sustaining, never napping; he does not sleep. Allah owns the kingdom of all in the heavens and all the earth."

The Christians have doubts, and they did not believe the prophet Muhamad, many Christians say, "the Messiah Jesus (Isa) is Allah!" According to Islamic resource, who has authority against Allah, if Allah, the creator of the universe, would like to destroy the Messiah Jesus (Isa) and his mother, Mary (Marium), and everyone on the earth? Allah is the honor of the heavens and the earth and everything in between. Allah creates what he wants. Allah has power over all things. What is worse than those who suffered the curse and anger of Allah? Allah transformed those into monkeys and pigs by his higher power. Those who worship evil are in the defiant rank and far away from the straight path. Do the people worship something that has no power to damage or benefit them? Allah hears and knows all things. The people of the holy books of Torah and the gospel should do not overdo the limits in their religions. And they should not violate the facts and should not follow the desires of people who were wicked in past times. Evil deceived people and made them lose themselves from the straight way. The evil deed and the righteous deed are not equal, even if the evil deed is a glare in the people's eyes. They should respect Allah, and they should understand so they can prosper. The people of the holy book have no base to stand on, unless they stand by the laws of the original gospel (Al-Ingeel), the original Torah, and all the original previous sacred books.

The rejecters among the children of Israel said, "Jesus (Isa) made obvious magic tricks."

According to the interpretation of Islamic resources, the parties of the children of Israel differed. On the Day of Resurrection, Allah will release to them their records. Allah, the creator of the universe, will punish those who differ in these stories, bestowing to his will. The Messiah Jesus (Isa) healed sick individuals by the permission of Allah and resurrected a dead person by the permission of Allah. He created a bird from dust by the permission of Allah. Jesus (Isa) told them how much they reserved in their houses by the permission of

Allah. The Messiah Jesus (Isa) prayed and asked Allah to send a table spread to the believers of the children of Israel after they asked him that. Allah accepted his prayer and ordered the table spread to be a feast. Allah raised the prophet, Jesus (Isa). to the heavens, and no one murdered him. Thousands of years, before Jesus (Isa) was born, Allah raised the prophet Enoch (Idris) to the heavens. No one tortured or slayed the Messiah Jesus (Isa).

The Jewish and Christians say, "if you are Jewish or Christian, you will be guided to salvation."

The religion of the prophet Abraham (Ibrahim) is the truth, and he did not join anything with Allah in worshipping. Will the Jewish and Christians debate with Muslims about Allah, the creator of the universe? Allah is the creator of all creatures. Muslims are responsible for their deeds, and the Jewish and Christians are responsible for their deeds. Muslims should be sincere in their faith to Allah.

The Christians say, "Allah, the creator of the universe, has a begotten son."

According to Islamic resources, Allah is self-sufficient. Allah created the heavens, earth, and everything in-between. Those do not have authorization for telling lies. They say about Allah what they do not know. Those who formulate lies against Allah will never prosper and will have little gratification in the life of this world. Then, they will return to Allah. He will make them taste the tough penalty for their disbelief of the truth. Allah made signs of Jesus (Isa) and his mother, the Virgin Mary (Marium); Allah protected them in a cave on a high mountain of rock, affording them rest and security with waterfall springs. Allah grants satisfaction to people who work in righteousness. He counts well all that they do. People used to worship humans or things, but that does not give them inspiration or grace. This thing or humans will reject their lies and become an enemy against them. Allah has set the evil ones against the unbelievers to exacerbate their rage. The prophet Muhamad did not rush against them. Allah counts and gives them a limited time.

According to the interpretation of Islamic resources, on the Day of Resurrection, Allah will gather the virtuous people to the gardens of Eden, like a band. And will drive the sinners to the fire of hell, like craving cows driven down to the water. None of them will have the power to resist. The Christians say that Allah, the creator of the universe has a begotten son. They say the most terrible thing: when they say that Allah has a begotten son, the skies want to shatter, the earth wants to fragment apart, and the mountains want to be flipped upside down because of their saying that Allah has a son. It is not compatible with the majesty of Allah to have a son. Every creature in the heavens, and the earth must come as a slave to Allah, the higher power. He counts all of them and has their number. Allah is the most merciful and gracious.

"Become Jewish or Christian to be guided," the people of the holy books said.

According to Islamic resources, people of the holy books should follow the religion of the prophet Abraham (Ibrahim); he did not associate with Allah. The people of the holy book should say such as Muslims—that they believe in Allah, the creator of the universe; in what was sent to them; in what was sent to Abraham (Ibrahim), Ishmael (Ismael), Isaac (Isehaq), Jacob (Yaqub), and the tribes (Al-Asabat), and in what was revealed to Moses (Musa) (Torah) and Jesus (Isa) (Gospel) and in what was brought to Muhamad (Quran). They should not distinguish between any one of the prophets or messengers, and they should submit their faith to Allah, the creator of the universe. Do the people of the holy book dispute with Muslims about Allah, the creator of the universe? He is creator of all people. Muslims are responsible for their behaviors, and the others are responsible for their behaviors. Many Muslims are faithful to Allah.

"No one will enter the eternal garden unless he or she is a Jewish or a Christian," the people of the holy books said to the prophet Muhamad.

According to Islamic resources, these are the wishes of the people of the holy books (Jewish and Christians). They should produce their proof if they said the truth. Whoever submits his or her faith to Allah, the creator of the universe, and forgives others will get a reward of the eternal garden. They will have no fear, and they will have no grief. If the people of the holy book love Allah, they should follow the messenger Muhamad. Allah will love them and forgive their sins. Allah is a forgiver and is merciful. If they turn away, Allah does not love those who do not believe or anyone who disputes in the matter of the Messiah Jesus (Isa), after the knowledge came. The prophet Muhamad had an order to invite Muslims' children and the holy book's children, Muslims' women and the holy book's women, and all people: then let all pray, and request a curse from Allah to the liars, amen. The people of the holy books, Torah and the gospel (Al-Ingeel) should have a word between them and Muslims that they all worship Allah, the creator of the universe, and do not associate anything. They should not take humans from themselves or other things to worship. If they turn away, bear witness that Muslims submitted their faith to Allah, the creator of the universe, in Islam.

Instruction and answers

People asked the messenger Muhamad, "what was his opinion on using alcohol and gambling?"

According to Islamic resources, the drinking of alcohol and gambling are profound sins. Using both cause hazards rather than gains.

People asked the prophet Muhamad, "what will happen for the human after death?"

According to the Islamic resources, there are two angels are seated next to every human, one on the right and one on the left. The human does not pronounce a word without observers; the angels write records. The coma of the death conveys the truth, which the human was trying to avoid. And when the trumpet blown, that will be the day of the promise that the human wanted to avoid. On the Day of Resurrection, the individual will come with an angel driver and an angel witness. Allah will remove the cover from the human's eyes, and the vision will focus like solid steel. If the human was neglectful, and spiritual careless; the angel will say, "these are the documents that I have of this human." And Allah created humans and knew that their personal emotions murmurs and distress their thoughts. Allah and the angels are close to them, more than the robe of their veins. The order of Allah will be to push the evil and his followers in the hellfire—those who unbelieved and prevented the upright manners, aggressors, liars, and those who associated another thing in worshiping of Allah. They will have the painful punishment. The evil one will say, "I did not make him or her a wrongdoer, but the human committed intense mischief." And it will be expected that Allah will say to them, "do not argue before me. I already cautioned you. I do not switch my words; I am not unjust for people." Allah will question the hellfire, "are you full?" It will reply, "are there any more humans and evil ones?" And the eternal garden will be near for the virtuous people.

"Why was the Quran not sent in other languages than Arabic?" the rejecters asked the prophet Muhamad.

According to the Islamic resources, the holy Quran is a guide and a healing to those who believe. But the unbelievers' ears are deaf, and their eyes are blind. They will be called from a distant place of hell. In whatever thing Muslims differ, they should turn it to the decision of Allah, the creator of the universe. The prophet Muhamad believed, and he turned to Allah. Allah established for people the same religion, which was revealed to the prophet Noah (Nuh). Allah commanded the prophet Abraham (Ibrahim), the prophet Moses (Musa), and the Messiah Jesus (Isa) that they should remain dedicated to the religion of Allah and make no divisions. Allah keeps the holy Quran from any change forever. The nearest people to the Muslims in affection are the Christians because among them ministers and pastors, who are not arrogant. when they listen to what was sent in the Arabic holy Quran; their eyes are tearing because of what they know of truth. Those Christians say, "we believe in Allah, the creator of the universe. Register us among the witnesses. Why did we not believe in Allah and whatever has come to us of truth? We ask forgiveness of Allah, and we ask Allah to admit us in the eternal garden with the virtuous people." Allah will reward those Christians for what they achieved. They will live forever in the eternal garden, which includes rivers, that will be the rewards of the virtuous people.

People asked the prophet Muhamad, "what turned the Muslims from the direction in which they were used to pray?"

According to Islamic resources, east and west are owned by Allah, and Allah guides who he wants to the straightway.

People asked the prophet Muhamad, "what about the new phases of the moon?" According to Islamic resources, the new phases of the moon are signs to mark periods of time for people and for pilgrimage timing.

Muslims asked the messenger Muhamad, "what was permitted for us to eat."

According to Islamic resources, it is permitted for Muslims to eat all pure (*halal*) things and to eat what they have hunted by the catch of birds. They can eat what they catch, but they should say the name of Allah, the creator of the universe, during processing of food and during eating. The forbidden foods are the pig meat and un-slaughtered meat and blood, and the drinking of alcohol. People should fear Allah because his punishment is quick.

Some Muslims asked the messenger Muhamad, "how should we spend the charity?"

According to Islamic resources, people should spend charity for parents, relatives, orphans, the needy, and the traveler. And whatever they do of good deeds, Allah knows.

People asked the prophet Muhamad, "what about the fighting in the four sacred months, in the Islamic lunar calendar (Ragab, Zo-Aqedah, Zo-Alhaji, Moharram)?"

According to Islamic resources, fighting in the sacred months is forbidden except for defense. In the sight of Allah, preventing the people from their arrival to the way of Allah to the sacred mosque and driving its people out are graver. Association with Allah is worse than killing people. The rejecters will not stop fighting the believers until the believers turn back from their religion. If anyone leaves the Islamic faith and dies as unbeliever, he or she works will not bear credit in this life or on the Day of Resurrection. The unbelievers will be companions of the hellfire and will live in it forever.

People asked the messenger Muhamad, "what is the spirit of the soul?"

According to Islamic resources, the spirit of the soul is by the command of Allah, and the people are given only a little knowledge.

People asked the messenger Muhamad, "what do we spend?"

According to Islamic resources, people should spend forgiveness on each other, and should ask forgiveness of Allah in life and after life.

People asked the prophet Muhamad, "what is the life span of humans?"

[And for every nation is a specified term. So, when their time has come, they will not remain behind one hour, nor will they precede it (The Quran Translation, Ali, Yusuf 2007, 7:34)].

According to Islamic resources, Allah created life span for every nation or creatures, when their terms end, they cannot live an extra-hour or live less than their term. The reasons of death varied, but the death has decreed on time.

The Rejecters of Makah

"Muhamad, you are a forger," the rejecters of Makah said.

The prophet Muhamad was commanded to serve Allah, and Allah made Makah city sacred. He got a command from Allah to be one of those who submitted his faith to Allah in Islam. Most people do not understand that the angel Jabril (Gabriel) brought the verses of the Quran to the prophet Muhamad. He reinforced those who believe. He was as an ideal and a glad tiding to the believers. According to the interpretation of Islamic resources, Allah ordered the prophet Muhamad to follow the religion of the prophet Abraham (Ibrahim) and not to associate.

The prophet Muhamad needed helpers, such as the Messiah Jesus

(Isa) said to his disciples, "who will be my helpers to the faith of the Allah?"

The disciples (Howarion) said to Jesus (Isa) "we are your helpers." A party from the children of Israel believed, and the other did not believe. Allah gave power to those who believed (the Christians) against the unbelievers of the children of Israel, and the believers succeeded.

Anger Management

The prophet Muhamad advised people to have patience in hardship. Patience is initiated from deep faith in the pure monotheism of Allah, the creator of the universe. The prophet Muhamad received verses to comfort feelings during distressed times. In the interpretation of Islamic resources, "did not Allah bless your heart? And he removed your burden that was weighing on your back. Allah raised your rank. So, with the tough conditions, there will be relief. With distress, there will be relief. If you have done with your labor, stand for further prayer to Allah and think in devoutness to Allah."

The five times prayers should be on the prescribed times, but the additional prayers can be done at any time.

The Muslims who are sincere to Allah will overcome hardship (distress) because their faith is such as a powerful waterfall that can damage a solid rock. Reading or listening to the Quran can calm down the person. All his life, the messenger Muhamad had good morals and honesty. His speech was authentic and honest. He was the best leader of groups. He had respectable leadership features and a decent character. Nowadays, political leaders, pastors, and counselors study the rules of group leadership and how to guide a group of people. The messenger Muhamad was a leader of thousands of Muslims. He succeeded by the guidance of Allah, the creator of the universe, to make sure that Muslims had cohesion and were united against the rejecters of Makah and their allies.

Reading or listening to the holy Quran supports people in

distressful situations. Reading or listening to the holy Quran alleviates emotional pain, guides the just, reassures worry, calms anger, and induces hope. The prayers help well-being, initiate happiness, facilitate times for self, and encourage the person to start over. All the heavenly religions came to the earth through angels to the messengers who received the words of Allah, except the prophet and messenger Moses (Musa), who talked directly to Allah.

Envy and Illness

The prophet Muhamad was a messenger of Allah to the humans and the jinn (invisible unseen creatures). At that time, there were numbers of jinn who listened to the Holy Quran. The jinn said, "we have listened to a wonderful Quran." The Arabic holy Quran includes words of Allah, protect humans from evil, envy, and harmful evil acts.

According to the interpretation of Islamic resources, "say, I seek protection by Allah (the creator of the dawn) from evil's hazard and from Satan of darkness. And from Satan (evil) who practices witchcraft when they blow in knots, and from of envy."

According to the interpretation of Islamic resources, "say, I ask protection of Allah (the creator of the humans), the king of the humans, the God of the humans. I seek refuge by Allah from the evil who whispers in the chest of humans and from jinn (unseen) and from humans."

The prophet and messenger Moses (Musa) went to show the pharaoh the sign of Allah when the magicians threw their witch crafts on the floor. The interpretation of Islamic resources, the prophet Moses (Musa) said, "whatever you have invented of witch crafts, Allah will stop all of it. Allah does not guide those who do exploitation." The people should ask protection of Allah from envy and Satan's witchcraft.

According to Islamic resources, the prophet Abraham (Ibrahim) said, "whenever I get sick, Allah cures me." And the prophet Job (Ayyub) prayed, "my Allah, I got harmed by the Satan (evil), and you are the most merciful." Allah answered his request and cured him. The people should ask Allah, the creator of the universe, for forgiveness and healing from illness.

The Prophet Muhamad's Wives

The prophet Muhamad waited years after the death of his first beloved wife, Khadijah, then he married a widow of his soldier. He also married a woman in slavery, Maria the Christian. And he married one of his relatives who had emigrated to Yathrib. The messenger Muhamad married them to help them to survive because there was no other one helping them. He wanted to be a formal helper to them. His best friend was Abu-Baker El Sediq, who gave his daughter Aisha to the messenger Muhamad as a future wife. The messenger Muhamad did not have a relationship with Aisha until she reached the age of puberty. Then, she expressed her desire to marry the prophet Muhamad. At that time, the age of marriage of all girls was around fourteen years old. Most the wives of the prophet Muhamad died during his life. He did not marry all of them at the same time. He might have four, and if one died, he married another one. At that time, the mortality rate was high.

In Makah, the air temperature was very hot, and there was violence between the Arab tribes. There was no medical treatment, and there was no civilization. Allah's commandments guided the prophet and messenger Muhamad. The prophet Muhamad asked his wives if they would like the brilliant life of this world and its glitter to come. He would give them fair rights and let them go with a good-looking separation for divorce. But they chose the rewards of the eternal garden. The prophet Muhamad had a problem with one of his wives because she said something against him. She asked him, "who did inform you." He said, "Allah informed me." Then, he made up with her after she apologized.

Victory at Makah

Allah granted victory to the prophet and messenger Muhamad

and the Muslims. The military of the messenger Muhamad had thousands of soldiers. They had Allah's permission to enter Makah. The soldiers surrounded Makah with their weapons and said, "Allah is the greatest." At Makah, there were still rejecters. The messenger Muhamad ordered his army to prevent bloodshed. The Muslims of Quraysh who had emigrated returned to their homes in Makah. Before Islam, the rejecters of Makah worshipped statues and idols. Most rejecters of Makah converted to Islam. The messenger Muhamad and the Muslims cleaned Al-Kabbah and the sacred mosque (*Haram Sharif*). They removed statues and images. Gradually, the number of Muslims increased. Now, there are more than 1.5 billion Muslims worldwide. The victory of Muslims at Makah was sent in the Quran. After that, the people of the Makah tribes and the surrounding tribes converted to Islam.

Invitation Outside Makah

The rejecters did not hope to meet with Allah, and they said, "bring us a holy book other than the Quran or change the Quran."

The messenger Muhamad had no authority to change the Holy Quran by himself. He followed what was sent to him from Allah. He obeyed Allah. He feared the penalty of the Day of Resurrection. He stayed among people of Makah for his entire life before this, and he was illiterate. Did the rejectors not understand? The messenger Muhamad invited people to Islam outside Makah village. He went with a few Muslims to Al-Taef city, which was located near Makah city. He invited groups of people to Islam, but they refused to change their minds. He invited the chiefs of Al-Taef, but they told the prophet to leave their city. The chiefs of Al-Taef ordered their servants to throw rocks at the messenger Muhamad and the Muslims. He also invited the tribes around Makah city, and they converted to Islam gradually. The prophet Muhamad asked Allah to help him. According to the interpretation of Islamic resources, Allah choose the believers who will walk on the straight path, on the Day of Resurrection. No one can confuse those people, and no one can help those who are not chosen by Allah. There is no God but Allah, and Muhamad is the messenger of Allah. Those who obey Allah, no one can change their minds. And those who lose the upright way, no one can straighten their way. The prophet Muhamad did not associate. No humans or evil could take him away from Allah's path. He found protection only in Allah's straightway. He did not know whether the promised punishment to the rejecters would be soon or appointed in a distant time. The prophet Muhamad invited people to the religion of Allah.

The Messenger Muhamad Died

In Saudi Arabia, many Arab tribes converted to Islam, but some people rejected it. The rejecters did not submit their faith to Allah. The prophet Muhamad conveyed the message to them in truth, but they turned their backs to the message of Allah, the creator of the universe.

Allah knows what open speech is, and what hidden speech is. Allah sent the Quran to the prophet Muhamad. Allah has the secrets of the heavens and the earth. He is he forgiver and merciful. Is the hellfire better than the eternal garden, which is a reward for virtuous people? After more than twenty years of inviting people to Islam, the prophet Muhamad died.

Khalifa Abu Baker El-Sediq

Muslims chose Abu Baker El-Sediq to be the leader (Khalifa). He said, my people: who worships the prophet Muhamad, he died, and who worships Allah; Allah is alive forever. He never dies.

Khalifa Omar Alkhatab

Omar was a strong man of the Quraysh tribe. Before the second emigration of Muslims, Omar wanted to kill the messenger Muhamad. He was angry and aggressive with his sister because she and her husband converted to Islam. Omar listened to his sister as she was reading the Quran. Omar slapped her face because she converted to Islam, but when he saw the blood on her face, he felt guilty. He asked her to give him the Quran to read.

Omar's sister said to him, "first, go to purify yourself with water." She gave him the Quran to read.

Omar converted to Islam; he went to the prophet Muhamad with his weapons and said, "there is no God but Allah, Muhamad is the messenger of Allah."

Quraysh tribes got angry because Omar converted to Islam. They asked Omar to return to their religion, but he refused. Omar was one of the best friends of the prophet Muhamad. After the death of the Khalifa, Abu-Baker, Omar became the Muslims' Khalifa. He was famous for his justice and honesty. Othman Ben-Affan was chosen as Khalifa after Omar's death. Then, Khalifa Ali Ben Abi-Talib was chosen after the death of Othman. No one will carry the mischief of others. Whoever is righteous, it is for himself or herself. On the Day of Resurrection, everyone will have his or her documented records, which were written by the guardian angels. Allah will grant forgiveness and the reward of the eternal garden to the virtuous believers, and Allah will decide the punishment of hellfire to the unbelievers. The fair avenue is the way of the righteous to Allah that people should choose.

CHAPTER 5

The Signs of the Creator of the Universe

ALLAH, THE CREATOR OF THE UNIVERSE HAS MANIFESTED SIGNS IN THE creation of every natural thing, such as water and plants. The plants not only serve as a source of food for humans, animals, birds, and insects, but they also produce oxygen that is used by most creatures during respiration. Allah created many plants that can help in curing illness. Examples of plants mentioned in the holy Quran are olives, figs, grapes, pumpkins, wheat grains, and palm dates. Those plants have proven evidence through extensive scientific research to have beneficial use to human health. The researchers of pharmacognosy subtracted compounds from plants and natural products used in manufacture of drugs.

Allah gives people honey from nectar, which is collected from flowers and produced in the abdomen of honeybees. Allah taught the honeybee to build cells in hills, in trees, and in homes and to eat of all the plants of the earth. After a cycle in their bodies, honeybees produce honey of assorted colors. According to Islamic resources, people can use it as a cure and healing of illnesses.

[And your Lord taught the Bee to build its cells in hills, on trees, and in (men's) habitations; then to eat of all produce

(of the earth) and find with skill the specious path of its Lord: there issues from within their bodies a drink of varying colors, wherein is healing for men: verily in this is a sign for those who give thought (The Quran Translation, Ali Yousef 2007, 16:68-69)].

Allah, the creator of the universe granted good health to the people. The physiological (normal) body functions of humans. These include all the organ systems, such as the cardiovascular, respiratory, digestive, endocrine, reproductive, and urinary, and nervous systems.

Thinking on the grace and mercy of Allah empower of Muslims' spirituality. Vision is one of the greatest graces of Allah, the creator of the universe. In Ophthalmology, visualization of objects starts from specialized receptors in the eyes that detect certain frequencies of visible light waves. Those receptors are called rods and cones. These cause a stimulus to pass through the retina, optic nerve, the optic tract, and the optic chiasma, and lateral geniculate nucleus (LGN). Then, it arrives at the visual center in the occipital cortex of the brain, where it can be interpreted as an image in the brain.

Hearing also is a great mercy of Allah. Sound waves are similarly transmitted to the temporal lobe of the brain through specialized structures in the ear, which include the eardrums, the bony ossicles in the inner ear, and the auditory nerve. It has ascending stimuli fibers and descending inhibitory fibers.

[He is Who has created for you (the faculties of) hearing, sight, feeling and understanding: little thanks it is you give! (Quran translation, Ali Yousef 2007, 23:78)].

Allah controls the lifespan of everything. He also gives people the grace of special senses, such as vision, hearing, taste, smell, and touch. Olfaction is directly through nasal receptors in the nose that transmit signals to the olfactory center in the brain. Olfaction is an essential component of the ability to smell and taste; taste receptors are present on the tongue papillae, and they are enervated by the glossopharyngeal and facial nerves.

In the skin, there are peripheral nerve endings for the sensation of pain, as a warning to and protection of the human body. There are also sensory receptors to feel cold, hot, fine, and crude touch. One of the mercies of Allah, the creator of the universe, that differentiates humans from other mammals is that humans have cognitive thinking about ideas. The higher-order processes of cognition, memory, and decision-making take place in parts of the brain, including the cerebrum, midbrain, thalamus, tegmentum, and hypothalamus.

Healthy people can use their lower limbs for movement and can use their hands for their fine-motor activities, such as writing, planting, cutting, sewing, constructing, cleaning, and working.

The most merciful Allah blessed humans and other creatures with the ability to communicate. The speech pathway starts with the movement of the tongue and the vocal cords by nerves that originate in the brain. The vocal cords open and close to produce appropriate sounds and words. Sound waves that reach the ear are interpreted as comprehensible speech in the brain. The vestibular membrane of the inner ear keeps balance.

Allah, the creator of the universe, created the digestive system to break down and absorb food and drinks. Humans are blessed with teeth that are useful not only for chewing food but also for cosmetic purposes. Swallowing food and drinks from the mouth to the pharynx and the esophagus without aspiration to the respiratory tract and the lungs are another blessing from Allah. The stomach contracts and secretes hydrochloric acid to digest food. In the small intestines, there are histologic cells to absorb ingested material and water. Gut bacteria line the digestive tract and aid in the further digestion of fiber and other substances not broken down by the human body.

The pancreas secretes enzymes and hormones to digest proteins, carbohydrates, and fats (example: insulin to metabolize glucose). The liver secretes bile to aid in fat, and it stores glucose in the form of glycogen. It can break the glycogen digesting down into glucose, as needed during periods of fasting. It also metabolizes ingested harmful substances and detoxifies them, so they will be excreted in the stool.

The mercy of Allah, the creator of the universe, manifested in the creation of the renal system. The glomerulus is the functional unit of the kidney. It filtrates by design to purify the blood, producing urine. Urine includes the extra fluids, electrolytes, and other elements that the body needs to excrete. Excretion of excess fluids and minerals by the kidneys is a great blessing. Those who have renal failure use artificial kidneys by being on dialysis.

The most graceful and merciful Allah created the cardiovascular system in the form of the heart, arteries, veins, and capillaries. The heart works to pump blood throughout the body. It takes the non-oxygenated blood from the body and pumps it to the lungs. The oxygenated blood returns to the heart to be sent back to the body. The freshly oxygenated blood travels to all the other organ systems via arteries and then returns to the heart afterward in veins. Both the heart and veins have valves to prevent flow back in the reverse direction. Arteries have thicker layers that can resist the high-pressure system of the heart's pumping.

Allah the creator gives grace, manifests in the respiration physiology which starts by contraction of the diaphragm for inhalation of air. The nose purifies the air in the nasal cavities and sinuses as it travels down in the airway to inflate the lungs. The alveoli are the physiologic units of the lung, where the exchange of carbon dioxide and oxygen in red blood cells occurs. Oxygen is needed for life. Carbon dioxide is exhaled by relaxation of the diaphragm. Respiration, like other physiologic processes, is regulated by the nervous system and is controlled by Allah's will.

The endocrine system involves hormones that coordinate processes in the human body. Examples of hormones include cortisone and epinephrine from the adrenal glands; triiodothyronine (T3) and thyroxine (T4) from the thyroid gland; follicular-stimulating hormones (FSH) and luteinizing hormone (LH) from the pituitary gland; gonadotropin-releasing hormone (GNRH) and thyrotropin-releasing hormone (TRH) from the hypothalamus, and insulin and glucagon from the pancreas. The pituitary gland also produces oxytocin, vasopressin, prolactin, growth hormone, thyroid-stimulating hormone (TSH), and adrenocorticotropic hormone (ACTH).

Scientists around the world have discovered that the real higher power is Allah, the creator of the universe. He manages the world's process of the life cycles of all creatures. The reproductive system in humans and in other creatures is a sign of the power of Allah. In a normal human, releasing the hormone GNRH from the hypothalamus stimulates the release of the follicular-stimulating hormone (FSH) and luteinizing hormone (LH) from the pituitary gland, stimulating the production of testosterone in males and the production of sperm. In females, follicular stimulating hormone and luteinizing hormone regulate estrogen and progesterone levels and regulate the menstrual cycle, which starts at puberty and ends during menopause. After fertilization, sperm ascends to the uterus and up to the fallopian tubes to fertilize the ovum that is released every month by the female's ovaries. Fertilization will occur and subsequently the formation of a zygote. Progesterone is secreted from the ovaries; later, the placenta helps the uterus to form layers, where the zygote will be embedded in the wall of the uterus. The divisions of the zygote form the placenta, the yolk sac, and the embryo is formed. In the embryonic sac, the growth and development of the fetus takes thirty to forty weeks. Then, the fetus is delivered into outside life through the birth canal or through cesarean section, as willed by Allah.

The power of Allah, the creator of the universe is manifested in the healing of the damaged living tissues that regenerate the damaged skin, muscles, organs, and bones, such as burns, wounds, and broken bones that can rejoin after fractures. Allah has the power to heal all the pathologic diseases and to cure body's cells from the pathogenic diseases. For example, Allah has the power to cure and heal the individual who has acute bacterial infections that cause pathogenic diseases such as pneumonia, whooping cough, and typhoid fever. Allah heals and cures individual who has acute viral infections that cause diseases such as pandemic influenza, measles, and infectious mononucleosis. Allah is the only one who heals and cures acute, chronic illness and all illness, such as kidney disease (glomerulonephritis), bronchitis, or cancer. During illness, people should have patience, and they should praise Allah, the creator of the universe, and ask him to heal their diseases. The medical treatments are tools that provide Allah's will. Allah heals people.

[And when I am ill, He (Allah) is who cure me (Translation of the Quran, Ali Yusuf 2007, 26: 80)].

The creation of blood and the immune system is an amazing miracle that is appreciated by any believers who study microscopic histology. Blood is made of white blood cells, red blood cells, platelets, and plasma. Red and white blood cells and platelets are formed in the bone-marrow. One type of white blood cells is lymphocytes, which play an essential part in human immunity through antibodies and other cells that control other immune cells. Lysozyme is an enzyme that also plays a crucial role for immunity. It is present in saliva and tears and has antimicrobial effects. The integumentary outer protective layer for humans includes the skin, nails, and hair. These are the first lines of defenses against germs and foreign objects.

The nervous system consists of two major divisions, central and peripheral. The central nervous system contains the brain and the spinal cord. The brain is formed by the cerebral cortex, midbrain, cerebellum, and the brain stem. The normal-functioning brain prevents spasticity of muscles by sending inhibitory impulses to them. In general, each hemisphere of the brain coordinates the contra lateral side of the body. For example, lesion affecting the left side of the brain causes spastic paralysis on the right side and should be diagnosed as a left upper motor neuron lesion.

Every center in the brain has an important function that coordinates the body. The medulla oblongata in the brain stem has centers that regulate vital organs, such as the heart and lungs. The medulla oblongata has nuclei of cranial nerves, such as The Vigus nerve, which is a vital nerve of the parasympathetic nervous system.

The peripheral nervous system includes motor neurons that facilitate muscle and skeletal motor functions, the enervation of organs, and the relay of sensory information. (Jacob and Franco 1966).

Allah the creator gives mercy that manifests in the creation of the muscle and skeletal system. In human anatomy, muscles, bones, and joints are crucial in body movement and flexibility. Muscle contractions and relaxations are parts of motion and relaxation of the body. The process of exercise helps contraction of muscles and joints. Body motions assist the metabolism and the circulation of the blood. The movement is organized and coordinated by the peripheral nerves that relay to the spinal cord. The ascending tracts carry the impulses from the spinal cord to the brain. Stability is coordinated by the cranial vestibular nerve, which has a relay from the brain to the internal ear.

In the parasympathetic nervous system, acetylcholine is secreted as the neurotransmitter to coordinate processes, including increasing digestion and decreasing heart rate. The sympathetic nervous system is regulated by epinephrine (Adrenalin hormone) and nor-epinephrine (nor-adrenalin hormone) that is secreted by the adrenal medulla of the suprarenal gland. Epinephrine is secreted during times of stress and creates fight-or-flight response, such as an increase in heart rate and increase in respiratory rate.

[And among His (Allah's) signs is the sleep that you take by night and by the day, and the quest that you (make for live hood) out of His bounty: verily in that are Signs for those who hearken (Translation of the Quran, Ali Yusuf 2007, 30:23)].

Humans cannot stay awake with full brain function for more than few days. Sleep is a crucial factor for memory. Sleep is divided into four stages. Allah, the creator of the universe, grants humans the ability to sleep. One must appreciate the blessing from Allah in the ability to continue spontaneous breathing while sleeping. Other involuntary processes in humans are regulated by the autonomic nervous system, which consists of the sympathetic and parasympathetic nerve centers.

[Remember in your dream Allah showed them to you as few if He has shown them to you as many, you would surely

have been discouraged, and you would surely have disputed in (your) decision: but Allah saved (you): for He knows well the secrets of (all) hearts (The Quran Translation, Ali Yousef 2007, 8:43)].

Dreams are one of the manifestations of Allah, the creator of the universe. Dreams occur during the third stage of sleep. In neurology, the fourth stage of sleep is referred to as a rapid eye movement stage (REM). Neurologic researchers show that an EEG of the brain during the REM stage is as active as when the person is awake, with rapid eyes movements that see successive images. During the dream, the person can see images, hear voices, act without movement, and talk without sounds. The person lives in an imaginary movie. If an individual is near the dreamer, he or she does not see or hear anything relating to the dream of the dreamer.

Allah, the creator of the universe, granted some people the ability to predict the future through their dreams, such as messengers. In Egyptian history, there was documentation, including that one of the kings of ancient Egypt had a dream about the future of Egypt for seven years. In the Quran, verses indicate that the prophet Joseph (Yusuf), the son of the prophet Jacob (Yacoub), interpreted the dream of the king of Egypt. The reality of dreams is more than human recognition.

Dreams sometimes reflect the feelings and thoughts of the person, or they may warn of something that will happen in the future. Some dreams are nightmares. Allah shows people a few things in their dreams. If Allah showed them more things, they would be discouraged and be unable to make decisions. Allah keeps the secrets of all hearts.

International scientists and researchers have proved that the world—physical, chemical, biological, social, or all sciences are under the control of the real higher power of Allah, the creator of the universe. For example, the natural magnetic field around the earth, the layers of atmosphere, which has oxygen, around the earth; the difference in atmospheric weather in the four seasons; and natural disasters are controlled by the real higher power Allah, the creator of the universe.

[Then which of the favor of your Lord will you deny? He
has let free the two bodies of flowing water, meeting together:
Between them is a Barrier which they do not transgress (the
Quran translation, Ali Yousef 2007, 55:18-21)].

The junction of the Nile River and the Mediterranean sea is one
of the manifestations of the higher power of Allah. The salty sea's
water does not transgress into the fresh-water Nile River. The pure
monotheism of Allah is proved in the perfection of both the solar
system and the microscopic world.

CHAPTER 6

$\mathscr{P}$revention of $\mathscr{S}$ubstance $\mathscr{A}$buse

RESEARCHERS HAVE PROVED THAT PEOPLE MISUSE THEIR HEALTH AND money on abusing hazardous addictive substances. Harmful effects occur due to dependence on addictive drugs or alcohol.

Additionally, other addictive substances include the nicotine in tobacco, inhalants, hallucinogens, gambling, excessive food consuming, sex abusing, prolonged exposure to the waves of the cyberspace or television programs, and workaholic, all cause negative consequences.

Etiological factors result from abusing addictive drugs and alcohol, such as: peer pressure, unnecessary medical prescriptions of addictive drugs, drinking alcohol, loneliness, psychological trauma, physical pain or incidents, post-traumatic stress disorder (PTSD), and chemical dependent families. Other common causes of emotional and physical distress lead to drug and alcohol addiction.

According to medical references, most hazardous addictive substances affect the central nervous system (CNS). Alcohol and narcotics are CNS depressants, while amphetamine is a central nervous system stimulant. The following is a summary of the adverse effects of common addictive substances.

Alcohol

Alcohol (Ethanol) is a widespread addictive organic chemical substance. It is prepared by fermentation of grains, such as corn, and sugar cane. It is prepared as a beverage after dilution and purification. Another form of alcohol is methanol; it is a toxic type of alcohol used as a solvent and a starting material in the manufacture of formaldehyde and acetic acid. There are other methods of organic chemistry to prepare alcohol, and it can be used as fuel for automobiles (McMurry 2007).

Alcoholic beverages are central nervous system depressants. The regular drinking of alcohol can cause mental and physical disorders. The side effects of alcohol include intoxication, alcohol-induced depression or anxiety, withdrawal symptoms, and dependence.

Hazardous Effects of Alcohol (Ethanol)

The severity of signs and symptoms of alcohol intoxication depend on the amount of consumed alcohol and the duration. Those who drink alcohol may suffer from tremors, seizures, insomnia, nausea, increased heart rate, hangover, blackout, high blood pressure, and agitation. In case of pregnancy, alcohol causes fetal alcohol syndrome.

Alcohol intoxication in high doses causes shivering, slurred speech, unsteady gate, vomiting, daze, and coma. Death of a heavy drinker of alcohol occurs due to aspiration of vomit, leading to fatal asphyxia. Prolonged abuse of alcohol causes chronic illness, such as a decrease of body fluid or dehydration; enlarged liver (hepatomegaly), or increased alkaline phosphates enzyme levels, which announces a liver injury, liver cirrhosis, or fibrosis. Alcohol abuse can cause increased blood lipid, esophageal varices, peptic ulcer, vomiting of blood (hematemesis), blood in the stool (Melina), unsteady gait, and impairment in memory. Co-occurrence (A psychiatric disorder plus addiction and abuse of substance); it is a common disorder in youth and young adults.

The withdrawal symptoms of alcohol can include agitation, nausea, vomiting, and grand- mal seizures. The hazardous effects of alcohol need immediate medical intervention.

Laboratory Tests

Testing the blood–alcohol level helps to determine the tolerance. The laboratory tests GGT and CDT are helpful in monitoring the amount of alcohol that was consumed by the person. These tests identify heavy drinkers who have intoxication.

Narcotics or Opioids

Narcotics or opioids are addictive substances from the opioid alkaloid of opium plant. They are depressants to the central nervous system. There are natural and synthetic narcotics. Natural narcotics are morphine, but codeine and heroin are synthetics. Narcotics or opioids are painkiller medicines that cause side effects, such as: tolerance, withdrawal symptoms, and dependence. Tolerance means that the effect of the medicine for treatment diminishes with the standard doses because of the block of various pain receptors. If a person increases the dose of narcotics or opioids, toxicities will occur. Overdosing is more dangerous than heavy weapons because it stops respiration.

Addicts frequently look for any reason to have pain medicine prescriptions from physicians or dentists. The toxic effects of opioid overdosing need immediate emergency intervention. The signs and symptoms of overdose are constriction of eye pupils and low respiratory rate. In case of severe toxicity, respiration may stop, and the patient will die, so the patient needs immediate medical intervention.

Cocaine

Cocaine is a white crystalline powder. It is a natural alkaloid derivative of the coca plant and is a brain stimulant. It causes irritability, restlessness, insomnia, anxiety, and dilatation of the eye pupils. It also causes increased heart rate, increased metabolic rate, rises in temperature, hallucinations, and increased blood pressure. Overdosing on cocaine can cause a brain hemorrhage, stroke, and upper motor neuron lesions.

Amphetamines

Amphetamine and crystal methamphetamine are synthetic stimulant compounds to the central nervous system. The adverse effects are anxiety, paranoia, aggressive behavior, loss of appetite, dilatation of the eye pupils, increased blood pressure, increased heart rate, and insomnia. Overdose can lead to strokes, brain hemorrhage, and convulsions. Sudden withdrawal of amphetamine causes depression and smooth muscle cramps. Withdrawal symptoms need medical treatment.

Benzodiazepine

Benzodiazepine is a minor tranquilizer. It is a sedative and a depressant to the physiological functions. It is dangerous when taken with alcohol or central nervous system depressants because it causes synergistic effects (increased CNS depressant). Side effects include fast tolerance, addiction, and withdrawal symptoms. If the Patients abuse it; this can induce toxicity in overdosing (Shargel 1997).

LSD, PCP, and inhalants

Those are other addictive substances that cause risk to the central nervous system and toxicity. LSD and PCP are hallucinogens that cause hallucinations and an upside-down condition.

Marijuana

Marijuana is a mixture of the parts of a plant called Cannabis sativa. It causes central nervous system depressant. It is a psychoactive compound. The active compound is called delta-9-tetrahydrocannabinol (THC). The buds of the female plant have the highest concentration of THC. Hashish is the secretion of the tops of female cannabis plants that were collected and dried.

The side effects of abusing marijuana are as follows: it impairs motor coordination, increases heart rate, increases blood pressure, causes hallucination, and, in prolonged use in high doses, causes memory loss or dementia. Also in prolonged use, it decreases testosterone hormone; it impairs fertility in men and suppresses the function of ovaries in women. If a pregnant woman uses marijuana, the fetus may have congenital anomalies.

Other Addictive Substances

These include Pattex adhesive, toxic mushrooms and fungus, and other toxic inhalants.

Barbiturate Abuse

Barbiturates are sedative/hypnotic medicines and CNS depressants. One of the active ingredients is sodium pentothal.

Ultrashort barbiturates, such as thiopental sodium, is used for induction of monitored anesthesia. It may cause apnea and laryngospasm and may cause death.

The side effects of short-acting barbiturates, such as secobarbital, and the adverse effects of long-acting, such as phenobarbital are: increased heartbeats (tachycardia), congenital anomalies of the fetus, nausea, vomiting, dizziness, muscle weakness, cyanosis, tolerance, and dependency. Sudden withdrawal can cause death. Barbiturates are used in the treatment of anxiety, insomnia, and convulsion.

Nicotine

Nicotine is present in tobacco plants that are processed by drying and fermentation of tobacco leaves for smoking or chewing. Nicotine in tobacco causes side effects, such as vasoconstriction, decreased appetite, high blood pressure, and habituation. The tar in tobacco smoking increases the possibility of heart attack, high risk of lung cancer, and asthmatic bronchitis. Smoking cigarettes causes a high mortality rate.

Negative Consequences of Addiction

Addiction to or dependence on drugs and alcohol leads to negative consequences. If individuals are addicted drugs, alcohol, or hazardous substances; they will lose valuable things. The loss can be to their health, relationships, jobs, or money. They may have to live in a shelter for the homeless. They can suffer from the absence of social support. They might neglect their education, weaken their health, abuse others, and neglect their partners and children or elderly parents. Dependence on drugs or alcohol can result in incarceration or confinement in prison due to inappropriate behavior, such as fraud, battery, domestic violence, assault, or DWI. Drug addicts and alcoholics have similarities because they share interests, feelings, thoughts, and behaviors. Most drug addicts and alcoholics are in denial toward their dependency. They are self-centered and emotionally numb. They may have feelings of grandiosity or be antisocial. They manipulate the people who help them. Their key issue is to get the addictive substance because they are chemically dependent.

Addiction Recovery

According to scientific and social research, the basic items of addiction recovery programs are detoxification, rehabilitation, referral to the next level of care, and follow-up. It is important for the person to stay in a controlled environment, such as an inpatient facility. During detoxification, individuals may feel dizzy from the medication. They prefer to stay in bed, but the staff will make them follow the schedule of the inpatient facility. Sometimes, individuals miss activities, but they are watched twenty-four hours a day. The medical providers manage the cases with scientific procedures and medical protocol.

The social team manages the cases with theories, techniques, and communication skills. They use the agency policies and procedures. Social services staff follow the professional code of ethics. If the addict or alcoholic also has a mental disorder, he or she may suffer from worry, anxiety, fear, disappointment, loss of trust, or obsession. He or she may see something invisible to others or develop a personality disorder, such as antisocial, borderline, or narcissistic personality or post-traumatic stress disorder—the standard criteria in the Diagnostic and Statistical Manual, fifth edition (DSM-V). The DSM-V has classifications, diagnoses, and criteria for mental disorders to help mental health professional clinicians to accomplish their work. Those clinicians are psychiatrists, psychologists, social workers, and counselors. The clinicians can identify the correct diagnosis with the written procedures of the medical protocol. The clinicians at recovery and prevention programs should explain the hazardous effects of the addictive substances.

Most addicts or alcoholics find themselves lonely in an unmanaged life. The distressful feeling of shame and guilt cause inappropriate results of abusing addictive drugs or alcohol. Furthermore, peer pressure may cause youth or young adults to abuse and trade drugs with dealers as one form of maladaptive behavior. Sometimes, addicts share their medicine to their friends and families. They have unwise thinking because they abuse addictive drugs and alcohol and commit illegal acts. The requirements for addict or alcoholic include temporary shelter, inpatient and outpatient clinical intervention, food bank supplies, unemployment insurance, social security or disability support, monthly income, housing, career planning, social support, and a sponsor. Group and individual counseling or therapy for alcoholics and addicts are important items in the treatment plan.

Scientific researchers acknowledge that addicts and alcoholics should not act like an ostrich—that is, they should not hide their heads in the sand. They should look inside themselves and count self-defects while pushing toward upright motivation. The addict should use coping skills for sobriety. Prevention of relapse can be achieved by staying away from the targets that cause craving. Addicts and alcoholics should have the freedom to choose their coping skills that help them to stay sober. Methods of therapy can help addicts and alcoholics; one of these methods is group therapy, especially cognitive therapy.

Cognitive Therapy

There are two famous cognitive theories. The first cognitive therapy was developed by Aaron Beck. The second, called rational-emotive cognitive therapy, was developed by Albert Alice. Gerald Corey wrote that both approaches are active, directive, limited in time, and present-centered. Both theories focus on insight therapy, which emphasizes recognizing and changing negative thoughts and maladaptive beliefs.

Beck's approach is based on the way people feel and behave; it is determined by how they perceive it and their experiences. The assumptions of cognitive therapy are that internal communication is accessible to internal self-analysis and that one's personal belief has highly personal meanings. Interpretation can be discovered by the person instead of being taught by the therapist. The goal of the therapy is to change the automatic thoughts, which changes a person's thinking. This helps the patient who has depression and anxiety (Corey 2001).

Rehabilitation Programs

Rehabilitation programs include case management or counseling. The empowering of spirituality is recommended, within the individual's freedom of choice. The correct spiritual meditations to the higher power, the creator of the universe, help to restore wisdom and sanity. Spiritual teams are preachers, pastors from churches, or religious staff. Until now, there has not been a trained spiritual team that empowers spirituality to individuals without bias to their values. Faith-based programs impose their inherited customs, heritage, and religion.

In faith-based programs, addicts and mentally ill clients are obligated to share the program's religious services and celebrations. Individuals who have different beliefs are obligated to pray in Jesus's name and share Christmas services and Easter celebrations.

The spiritual team should not impose their values or religions. And they should not obligate the individuals to participate in their services, as individuals might have problems that originated from the faith-based programs.

In the faith-based programs, addiction management teams concentrate on directing the addicts and alcoholics to address the higher power to help them in correcting their unmanaged life. In Christian faith-based programs of addiction recovery, the treatment teams identify the name of the higher power as the Messiah Jesus (Isa). This explanation causes confusions to individuals who know that the Messiah Jesus (Isa) was a human and messenger of God (Allah). Christians and Muslims believe that the higher power created Jesus in the Virgin Mary without any man. So, the real higher power is not the Messiah Jesus. The Messiah Jesus (Isa) and the Virgin Mary (Marium), his mother, ate food and walked. Jesus is not the real higher power; he was not the creator of the universe. The believers in heavenly religions know that the real higher power is the creator of the heavens, earth, and everything natural in between.

In cases of addiction and mental illness management, the treatment team—social workers, ministers, and pastors of churches—should not obligate individuals to share the team's religious services and celebrations. The US Constitution includes freedom of choice. The spiritual team should clarify the objective of spiritual meditations, such as healing of unpleasant feelings, correcting irrational feelings and thoughts, and correcting maladaptive behaviors. The non-obligatory meditations in the name of the creator of the universe help with healing the body of sickness and help people in managing daily distress.

People who have good faith in the creator of the universe can manage their daily suffering, and they can start over. They can feel satisfied because they do their parts as they can. They can follow the righteous. There are four stages of forgiveness:

(1) forgiveness of the real higher power to the human.
(2) forgiveness of the disowned self to the real self.
(3) forgiveness of the self to others.
(4) forgiveness of others to self.

In Christianity, the pastors tell the Christians to love their enemies. In fact, loving the enemy can come after forgiveness of the enemy. On the other hand, some pastors spread hate toward the diverse faiths of others. They do not implement what they say. Developing sincere feelings can be directed toward Allah, the creator of the universe. After that, empathy and love can be developed toward self and others.

Long-suffering from alcoholism and addiction to hazardous substances will be the turning point for the addict or alcoholic. When consuming drugs or alcohol, people lose control over their behavior and thinking. They lose the ability to manage being easy going with their manipulative friends. They may fall into illegal and immoral issues under the influence of drugs and alcohol. Addicts and alcoholics cannot recognize the real higher power until they hit bottom because they live unmanaged lives. They conclude that they need the support of the real higher power to manage their lives. They will know that the support of the real higher power, the creator of the universe, guides them to the direction of sobriety and empowers hope and motivation.

In Islam, the real higher power is Allah, the creator of the universe. Intoxicants (alcoholic drinks) are forbidden. Gambling also is forbidden. And advised to leave this addictive substance to succeed.

[O you who believe! intoxicants (alcoholic drinks) and gambling, (dedication of) stones and (divination by) arrows are an abomination Satan's handwork: eschew such that you may prosper (The Quran translation, Ali, Yusuf 2007, 5:90)]

Management by prayers

No obligation in religion, but people can manage their low self-esteem and negative self-image by practicing regular prayer to the higher power, the creator of the universe; this is an effective behavior. Prayer can assist in the primary roles of peoples' lives, which direct their feelings, thinking, and behavior toward wisdom. Regular practice of the proper spiritual prayer assists in discovering hidden interests. Prayer empowers people to think of the creator of the universe. Prayer helps people to practice sincere faith in the creator of the universe. It alleviates anxiety, reinforces peace, and implants hopes. People ask the creator of the universe to help them. In fact, prayer produces assurance and self-confidence, which reflects a feeling of satisfaction. Then, the individual can cross the safe river's trail to walk on the fair avenue of peace.

There are Islamic centers around the world for anyone who is interested to visit. If anyone wants to know more, he or she can search for websites with valid and reliable information about the Holy Quran.

REFERENCES

1. American Psychiatric Association's (2013). *Diagnostic and Statistical Manual of Mental Disorder (5ᵗʰ Ed., DSM-5),* American Psychiatric Publishing, Arlington, Virginia.
2. Ali Yusuf Abdulah (2007). *The Qur'an Translation. Elmhurst,* 19ᵗʰ Ed. Tahreek/Tarsal Qur'an, Inc., New York.
3. The Nobel Quran, https://quran.com/
4. BMC, research in progress, https://biomedcentral.com
5. Brammer Robert (2004). *Diversity in Counseling,* Thomson Learning/Broke/Cole, Inc., Belmont, CA.
6. Capozzi David and Douglas R. Gross (2005). *Introduction to The Counseling Profession* (4ᵗʰ Ed), Pearson Education, Inc., Baston, MA.
7. Cory Gerald (2001). *Theory and Practice of Counseling Psychotherapy,* 6ᵗʰ Ed., Wadsworth/Thomson Learning, Inc. Belmont, CA.
8. Cory Marianne Schneider, and Gerald Corey. *Groups Process and Practice, 6ᵗʰ Ed.,* Wadsworth/Thomson Learning, Inc., Belmont, CA.
9. Delgado Jaime N., William A. Remer's, *Wilson and Griswold's (1998). Textbook of Organic Medicinal and Pharmaceutical Chemistry.* Lippincott Williams & Wilkins, Inc., Philadelphia, PA.
10. Flores, Philip J. (1997). *Group Psychotherapy with Addicted Populations,* Haworth Press, Inc., Binghamton, New York.
11. Haneef Suzanne (1996). *What Everyone Should Know about Islam and Muslims,* Kazi Publications, Inc., Chicago, IL.
12. Jacob Stanley W., and Clarice Ashworth Franco (1974). *Structure and Function in Man,* 3ʳᵈ Ed., W. B. Saunders Company, Inc. Philadelphia.

13. Kaufman Gershan (1991). *Shame: The Power of Caring, 3rd Ed.,* Shenkman Books, Inc., Rocher, Vermont.

14. Mader Sylvia S. (1985). *Biology: An Inquiry into Life,* 4th Ed., Wm. C. Brown Publisher, Dubuque, Iowa.

15. McCurry John (2007). *Introduction into Organic Chemistry.* Brokes/Cole Cengage Learning, India Biding House Inc. India.

16. Mohammed bin Ali bin Ibrahim Al-Arfaj and Abdul-Aziz bin Abdullah bin Baz. (2003). *Explanation of Important Lessons (For Every Muslim),* Darussalam, Huston, New York.

17. Nabil Abdul Salam Haroun (2005). *Teach Your Self Islam,* Dar An-Nashr, Cairo, Egypt.

18. Nicholas Michael P., and Richard C. Schwartz (2004). *Family Therapy Concepts and Methods* 6th ED., Pearson Education, Inc., Boston, MA.

19. Raven Peter H., and George Johnson (2002). *Biology.* McGraw-Hill Primes Custom Publishing, Inc., NY.

20. Schiraldi Glen R. (2000). *The Post Traumatic Stress Disorder Source Book.* 2000, Lowell House/NTC Contemporary Publishing, Inc., Los Angeles, CA.

21. Shargel Leon, Alan H. Munich, Paul F. Souney, Larry N. Swanson, and Lawrence H. Block (1997). *Comprehensive Pharmacy Review,* 3rd Ed., Williams & Wilkins/A Waverly Inc., Media, Pennsylvania.

22. Schiraldi Glen R. (2000). *The Post Traumatic Stress Disorder Source Book.* 2000, Lowell House/NTC Contemporary Publishing, Inc., Los Angeles, CA.

23. Siegelman Carol K., and Elizabeth A. Rider (2003). *Life-Span Human Development.* Wadsworth/Thomson, Inc., Belmont, CA.

24. Starr Cecie and Ralph Taggart (1992). *Biology: The Unity and Diversity of Life.* 6th ed., Wadsworth Publishing Inc., Belmont, CA.

25. Stanley L. Weinberg (1967), *An Inquiry into the Nature of Life.* Allyn and Bacon, Inc., USA.

26. Tamir Abu-Suod Mohammed, Noha Kamal Ed-Din Abu Al-Yazid (2001). *Biographies of the Rightly Guided Caliphs.* Edited by Ibrahim Kamara and Joan McEwan. Dar Al-Menorah Publishing, Inc., Egypt.

27. Latest Medical mews, https://medescape.com/

28. https://www.medicinenet.com/

29. https://www.webmd.com

30. https://www.merckmanuals.com/home/health-topics

31. Healthline: Medial information, https://www.healthline.com/

32. https://www.mayoclinic.org./

33. Medical App, https://www.drugs.com/apps/

ABOUT THE AUTHOR

The author is a licensed medical doctor of Physical Medicine and Rheumatology at Egypt. She moved and graduated with master's degree, arts of substance abuse counseling, ULM, USA. She worked a supervisor of mentally ill facility, Monroe, LA. Then, social service counselor (3), intern, southern Oak's addiction recovery. She was provisional LPC from 2007-2019, a member of ACA and a writer in (examiner.com). She wrote, Bridge to joy is reachable.

Printed in the United States
by Baker & Taylor Publisher Services